New Design
in the
Teaching of English

MARY COLUMBRO RODGERS

Trinity College, Washington, D.C.

INTERNATIONAL TEXTBOOK COMPANY

Scranton, Pennsylvania

The International Series in

SECONDARY EDUCATION

Consulting Editor

JOHN E. SEARLES

The Pennsylvania State University

To my husband and colleague,
DANIEL RICHARD RODGERS

Foreword

This book is appropriately titled *New Design in the Teaching of English*. It is the first attempt—a long-needed one—to view the teaching of English in its total context from the kindergarten through the graduate school; the author has boldly confronted the problem of sequence in its fullest sense. It is the most careful definition of the structure of English yet to emerge, a definition that accomplishes, among other things, a necessary identification of the relationship of *public communication* to the English curriculum in schools and colleges.

New Design is legitimately new in a special sense: it is the product of research and rigorous preliminary trial. Well known for her interest in research and her devotion to it as the basis for decisions of the profession, the author has brought a rich background of research to her work, and the book has been tested in a number of undergraduate and graduate courses which the author teaches.

New Design in the Teaching of English will be catalytic in the continuing dialogue of the profession. No matter what the reactions of individual readers to its specifics, the book is worth the serious attention of prospective and practicing teachers of English and of all students of the English curriculum.

Dwight L. Burton
The Florida State University

Preface

The teaching of English is an exciting commitment today. Whether at the elementary, secondary, college, or graduate level, English education is characterized by innovation and change. While old theories, models, and methods are in turmoil, new philosophies, paradigms, and procedures are in gestation, and hardly a day goes by that has not produced some new insight into the teaching of English. Modern research in English education, experimentation in English curriculum, and new linguistic data bring novelty and challenge to a tradition-bound discipline. As we look toward the future of the English teaching profession, tomorrow replicates the excitement of today. Computerized research in the humanities, nationally tested curriculum designs, and regional information retrieval centers all promise to keep English teaching at an apogee of fervor.

Incessant change, however, can be disturbing; excitement can frustrate creative effort. There seems to be a danger that both young teachers entering the profession and experienced teachers at every educational level might be hampered by change rather than exhilarated by it. Unless a teacher is secure in fundamental knowledge of his subject matter, he can be threatened by the recursiveness of change. The effective English teacher must have an all-around knowledge of his discipline in order to make wise judgments in teaching his subject matter. He cannot teach English well at any level unless he sees his commitment in relation to the total reality of the discipline and the needs of the students. It is by knowing the basic, substructural make-up of this subject that the English educator can make astute decisions about various kinds of emphases in information and skills, as well as the inclusion or exclusion of ever new facts, materials, and methods in his work. The English teacher who takes time to learn the fundamental, *underneath* structure of his discipline insures his professional orthodoxy.

Teaching English successfully in a pluralistic society is necessarily a challenging commitment. One of the humanities, English has traditionally been concerned with values. If a teacher ignores the value orientation of his discipline, he slights his humanistic commitment; if he accepts the value implications of his discipline, he faces the task of communicating these values to a diverse, multivalue society of students. The English curriculum designer, whether classroom teacher or curriculum specialist, can never hope for an *ultimate* English curriculum guaranteed to perpetuate the best in the Western literary tradition. Values, like all realities, change. Today's international communication requires the consideration of values thought *foreign* only a decade ago. In the United States of America, where the law of the land guards cultural diversity, it is necessary to implement a diversified English curriculum if students are to be trained for American democratic life.

New Design in the Teaching of English presents a pattern of the basic substructure of the English discipline. Once this design is studied and understood, any English educator, whether elementary, high school, or college teacher, graduate professor, or curriculum specialist can create a useful, coherent English curriculum for a given group of students. Each curriculum will be different, of course, depending on the philosophies of the designers and the needs of the students, but each curriculum will be the same in its basic structural organization. It is only by defining the fundamental design of the discipline called *English* that educators can achieve any consensus of opinion regarding subject matter and methods in the teaching of English. Such a definition *standardizes* the basics in the discipline and gives the individual educator *freedom to create* whatever curriculum structures and teaching strategies his philosophies and the needs of his students dictate. Such a definition also provides categories for new information before it is discovered. By reference to the categories, the English teacher can continually integrate new knowledge with old in a systematic way. The ignorance of a small body of new information in one segment of the discipline need not disorganize a teacher whose curriculum is firmly based on what has long been known in the total discipline.

New Design also traces the major role of the basic English components in the total K-Ph.D. education of native speakers. The rationale for the role is derived from the relationships of the components to one another. In some instances the relevance of the structural relationship to the needs of students is shown, but this is given only by way of example. Relevance of subject matter, like values, undergoes change. Planning strategies to communicate the relevance of any part of the English discipline is the work of the individual teacher who is close to his students and who can accurately assess their genuine needs.

Furthermore, *New Design* presents a theory of structured integration among the components of the English discipline. The mode is cross-component; the method is recursive. In a discipline whose components are self-integrated, decisions regarding the exclusion of subject matter can easily be made. English teachers need not fear the creative challenge of an ever changing discipline if they are knowledgeable in the basic components of their discipline, if they understand the relationship of the components to one another, and if they can integrate the components with each other. According to the rationale of *New Design,* the beginning teacher is a miniature of the expert practitioner; the daily lesson is a microcosm of the discipline; the year's syllabus is a facsimile of the K-Ph.D. program.

New Design in the Teaching of English has been used experimentally since 1964. Major concepts were used in the English teacher preparation program at the University of Rome, 1964–65, with nonnative speakers. A prepublication edition was tested for one year as the basic text in the specialized English methods course at the University of Maryland, 1965–66. In the Maryland experiment, sixty-one graduating English majors preparing to teach English in grades 7–12 were involved. The same edition was used experimentally in a graduate course in English curriculum and methods for experienced teachers of grades 5–14. A revision of the first prepublication edition was used as one of two basic texts in the NDEA Summer English Institute in Advanced Composition and Rhetoric at the University of Maryland, 1966. Here fifty English teachers, grades 9–12, with a minimum of five years experience were involved.

The present text is under further experimentation (1967-68) in the clinical school English program at Abraham Lincoln Junior High School, Washington, D.C. Here six graduate English interns in the Master of Arts in Teaching Program at Trinity College, Washington, D.C. are developing and teaching English units and daily lesson plans which implement the multicomponent, self-integrated concepts of *New Design.* Evaluation of the experimental program assesses both the effectiveness of *New Design* as a conceptual strategy for training teachers of urban children in grades 7–9 and the effectiveness of *New Design* as a methodology that improves children's total language arts performance.

In all, this book has been used as a teacher training text at the college and graduate school level for four years with 143 English teachers and supervisors. Evaluative responses of these persons who worked at fifteen grade levels (K-14) were carefully considered in preparing the final manuscript.

The present text is a revision of the prepublication manuscript. Considerable historical information relevant to linguistics, rhetoric, and the mass media has been eliminated. An appendix containing excerpts from the rhetorical treatises of Aristotle, Cicero, and Quintilian has been dropped. Only information related to the structure and implementation of the multicomponent, self-integrated English discipline has been kept.

Research for *New Design in the Teaching of English* was supported by The Ohio State University Summer Scholarship Program, a Fulbright-Hays Teaching Fellowship grant, the District of Columbia Public Schools, Trinity College, and the Ford Foundation.

Since *New Design* is an *experimental definition* of the K-Ph.D. English curriculum, the author welcomes academic and professional dialogue from K-university teachers who use the book in some way to provide more meaningful English education for America's youth. A supplementary text with diagrams and tables based on statistical results of the clinical school experiment is in preparation. *New Design II* will also include model units, and model daily lesson plans (with a description of experimental conditions related to the structures, and with an analysis of evaluative measures) useful to English teachers implementing the K-Ph.D. multicomponent, self-integrated curriculum.

Let us hope that the present edition of *New Design* will be useful as an organizational structure for continued research in the teaching of English and for improved daily lesson structuring in English.

A multicomponent, self-integrated curriculum is recommended to every English educator who cherishes both the subject matter of his discipline and his own creative power to structure significance for his students.

MARY COLUMBRO RODGERS

College Heights Estates, Maryland
March, 1968

Acknowledgments

The author is grateful to many professional friends who were instrumental in bringing this work to completion. Wilfred Eberhart, Paul Klohr, and Francis Lee Utley of The Ohio State University read the original manuscript and made valuable suggestions. Frank Zidonis, Ohio State University, served as mentor and consultant in applied linguistics, and John Portz, University of Maryland, helped to give final form to the first chapter. John Kean, University of Wisconsin, read the final manuscript, providing editorial comment.

Mrs. Priscilla Frasher, Mrs. Carolyn Miller, and Mrs. Marjory Malkin typed the revisions of the manuscript. Mrs. Ann Ferguson prepared the final copy. Kenneth Seamon, doctoral candidate in industrial education at the University of Maryland, prepared the majority of the illustrations.

The author is also grateful to the many experienced English teachers and supervisors who evaluated the experimental editions of *New Design,* tested the ideas in the classroom, and answered questionnaires providing feedback for revision.

Mention is due to Roland Goddu, Trinity College, Washington, D.C., who contracted the staff and resources of James C. Gillis, Jr., Quality Educational Development, Inc., Washington, D.C., to evaluate *New Design* as a conceptual strategy in training English teachers for disadvantaged children in grades 7–9.

Acknowledgment is also due to the English education majors at the University of Maryland and to the graduate English interns at Trinity College whose questions and feedback shaped *New Design* into a slimmer and more useful text at both undergraduate and graduate levels. Trinity interns who earned recognition for outstanding cooperation in the Trinity/Lincoln/Ford research project include the following: Julia Collins (Los Angeles, California), Mary Morrow Hollander (District of Columbia), Eileen Gevins (Baltimore, Maryland), Mary Ann Moran (Brooklyn, New York), Paula Peppler (Hyattsville, Maryland), and Joanne Vassallo (Harrison, New York).

The author also wishes to acknowledge the cooperation of ten experienced teachers and language arts specialists from K-12 schools in Washington, D.C. These persons were identified as educational leaders by Mrs. Charlotte Brooks, supervising director of English in the District of Columbia, and they were instrumental in testing *New Design* methodology for its value as an inservice teacher education strategy. After studying the methodology for one semester, each experienced educator conducted an individual research study of the effect of *New Design* methods on the total language arts improvement of selected children in D.C. schools. These persons include the following: Bernice Elam, Gretchen Gail, Douglas Gordan, Nellie Lawson, Jeanne Lea, Thelma Montgomery, Novella Phifer, Catherine Phynes, Alma Rimmer, and Donald White.

The author further acknowledges the cooperation of administrative/ supervisory personnel at Abraham Lincoln School who cooperated in the implementation of the research program that tested *New Design:* Mrs. Annie Jenkins, area English supervisor; Gilbert Diggs, principal; Louis Hartman and Mrs. Julie Mattingly, assistant principals.

Finally, the author is grateful to Mrs. Daniel Robert Rodgers whose care for little Robert makes professional commitment a pleasure.

MARY COLUMBRO RODGERS

Contents

List of Illustrations

Introduction

In his book, *The Aims of Education and Other Essays,* Alfred North Whitehead points out that the first intellectual task that confronts the infant is learning how to speak. It is an appalling task, requiring the correlation of meanings with sounds—and yet, by the time a child is two years of age he has made great strides in his journey toward mastery of the spoken word. Then, when he enters the first grade, he is asked to grapple with the awesome complexities of acquiring written language, that is, to correlate sounds with shapes, to extract meaning from little black squiggles on a white page. Good heavens! Have educators gone mad? They are asking a six-year-old child to perform mental operations that might well daunt a learned man after a lifetime of study. But again, by some miracle of learning, the child in a few months' time is able to open a book and decipher the meaning of printed words and to draw on paper the symbols that represent ideas of his own.

Man is a mysterious creature, and there is nothing more mysterious about him than his ability to use spoken words and written words, those shadowy symbols of the real world in which he lives and moves and has his being. He sees oaks, maples, and firs and he basks in their shade; he hears the rustle of their leaves, and he uses their wood to make a chair or a house; he employs the word *trees* to stand for the millions of tall, branching, bark-covered objects that rise to the sky in all the forests of the world. He tames electricity and manufactures scores of appliances that make life easier and more pleasant in his home; he calls them *refrigerators, washers, driers, radios, television sets, air conditioners, lights, electric ranges.* He speculates about himself, his place in the universe, and his relations with his fellow men, and he juggles the great abstractions of philosophy, religion, and political science; he talks of *being, purpose, the universe, eternity, God, government, justice, liberty,* sometimes without being sure that he understands what the terms mean. By means of language he comes into his heritage as a member of organized society and develops an awareness of the past, the present, and the future. He uses language as the instrument of thought. He becomes, in short, a *human* being—*homo sapiens.*

Learning about language is a lifetime process. It begins with the infant's birth cry and ends only with the last thought that floats through the individual's dimming consciousness or the last whisper he utters in the final hour of his existence. Between these two moments there stretches the span of human experience—all the activities of seeing, listening, doing, learning, reading, working, playing, struggling, dreaming, failing, and succeeding that life encompasses. Running along with these activities, like the instrumental accompaniment to a song, is the process of language learning. Here is the round, brightly colored object that rolls along the floor, and there is the word *ball,* which the child first hears and then speaks. Here is the rectangular, glass-sided container with its fish and seashells, and there is the word *aquarium.* Here is the crowded stadium on a fall afternoon, and there are the words *quarterback, split end, forward pass, touchdown.* Here is the rocket resting on its pad, and there are the terms *astronauts, space travel, Mars, the solar system.*

The English program in the schools and colleges of America is, as Professor Mary Columbro Rodgers brings out in *New Design in the Teaching of English,* basically the organized attempt of society to give direction, purpose, and system to the process of language learning. Life has already taught the kindergarten child a great deal about language, but there remains a great deal more to be learned. He understands what his parents, his friends, or his teacher says to him, but will he know what a television newscaster means when he speaks about "moderate casualties" or "the de-escalation of the war effort"? The five-year-old readily uses conjunctions and prepositions, participles and gerunds, compound declarative sentences and complex interrogative sentences, but, like the Frenchman who was surprised to discover that he had been speaking prose all his life, he would probably be startled to learn that such formidable terms could be used to describe his own utterances. Should the language arts program in the kindergarten and primary grades aim at helping the child to expand his vocabulary? If so, how? Through storytelling, through songs, through games, through talking about familiar but unnoticed things in the classroom, through walks through the neighborhood, through trips to stores and fire stations and post offices? At what grade level should instruction in grammar be introduced? What kind of grammar should be taught—traditional grammar, structural grammar, or transformational grammar? What, exactly, is the content of the proposed grammar? What are the precise purposes that it is designed to serve? Similarly disturbing questions can be raised about the instructional program in English for secondary school, for college, and for graduate school. What is the most efficient and economical way to teach spelling, punctuation, capitalization, sentence structure, and acceptable grammatical usage? How much stress should be placed upon written composition, or upon the study of rhetoric as a scholarly discipline? Should the strengths and the weaknesses of the mass media be explored or ignored? What is the proper balance between the literature of the past and present? Should the literature program be organized by chronology, by literary type, or by theme? Should some literature not be "studied" at all, but just read, enjoyed, and discussed briefly, as it so often is outside of school? How much attention should be given to English literature, to American literature, to world literature?

To raise questions such as these is to indicate the need for some fundamental agreement among English teachers at all levels regarding the scope of their subject matter and the functions it serves. It would be a tremendous step forward, for example, if the English teachers of the nation could select delegates to a kind of constitutional convention and instruct them to remain assembled until they agreed upon answers to the kinds of questions that Professor Rodgers raises in this study. Among the questions that this convention might well take up would be the following:

1. *Should the subject of English be conceived of as a long-range program extending from kindergarten through graduate studies leading to a Ph.D. degree?*

It seems reasonably clear at the present time that we have a fragmented rather than a unified program. There are all kinds of barriers to communication among teachers at different levels, and there are often curious omissions, duplications, and contradictions found in the courses offered in a single school or college English department. The materials and methods employed by the first-grade teacher are markedly different from those of the sixth grade teacher; the literature read in a junior high school program may seem trivial and inconsequential to a twelfth-grade teacher accustomed to teaching a *Beowulf* to Auden survey course in English literature. The university professor who offers a graduate seminar in the writings of Geoffrey Chaucer lives in one world; the young instructor who teaches three five-hour courses in freshman composition lives in another. And yet the question must be asked: Are there not certain interests and concerns that all these teachers share in common? Are there not certain common patterns woven on the loom of language, regardless of the room in which the shuttle is at work?

2. *Does the subject matter of English consist of four major components, namely literature, composition, linguistics, and the mass media of communication?*

Of these four components, literature and composition are well-established elements in programs at all levels. Linguistics, in the sense of attention to such fundamental elements as spelling, punctuation, capitalization, sentence structure, and acceptable grammatical usage, seems to be an unvarying concern in English programs at all levels; linguistics, in the academic sense of a study of phonetics, phonemics, morphemics, morphology, syntax, semantics, and transformational grammar, has been found chiefly in advanced undergraduate and graduate programs in English. At the present time its influence is being felt in secondary school programs, especially in the form of a study of transformational grammar, and to some extent in elementary school language arts programs. The mass media of communication are a pervasive influence in the lives of the overwhelming majority of Americans, and the National Council of Teachers of English has long urged that the study of television, radio, motion pictures, magazines, and newspapers be regarded as an essential part of a well-rounded English program. Many courses of study have suggested techniques and approaches that may be utilized in the effort to help young people become thoughtful, discriminating, and judicious users of these varied media of communication and entertainment. There probably still are some pockets of academic resistance to the idea of devoting class time to the examination and study of the mass media, but there appears to be a general recognition that youth needs training in the art of evaluating the accuracy and objectivity of a newscast, the quality of acting and story line found in a motion picture, and the level of writing found in widely read magazines and newspapers.

3. *Should the English program be regarded as containing both science components and art components?*

It seems reasonable to suggest that there are two basically different components in an English program, one of which may be called the science component and the other the art component. The science component consists of bodies of subject matter established by scholarly research and inquiry, such as the history of the English language, the various grammars of English, the history of literature, literary criticism and analysis, and communication theory. The art component, on the other hand, is epitomized by the act of composition, in which the student calls upon all his linguistic skills to do a piece of writing, to express his ideas orally, to read critically and thoughtfully, or to evaluate the literary merits of a poem, a play, or a work of fiction.

These three questions serve to suggest the general framework, or conceptual structure, purposed for the subject matter of English. It is a distinctive approach and a challenging one. The author does not seek to describe, grade by grade, what should go into an English program, but sketches in broad outline the general characteristics of a curriculum in English that takes into account both the great wealth of literature that poets, playwrights, essayists, and novelists have created through the centuries and scholarly studies of critics, rhetoricians, linguists, and literary historians. It is evident that in her own study, research, and teaching, she has caught glimpses of a light that never was on sea or land. Through this book, others may come to see this light also.

Wilfred J. Eberhart
The Ohio State University

1

The English Curriculum:
Conceptual Theory
and Implementation

English educators generally agree that a structured curriculum in the teaching of English is a K-Ph.D. (kindergarten-doctoral) construct. This means that from the organized language experiences of the nursery school child through the final oral examination of the doctoral candidate, the student has been the recipient of a planned English program. Until recently, English curriculums were segmented, usually consisting of kindergarten, elementary, and high school programs, general freshmen courses, undergraduate English major programs, master's, and doctoral programs. Today, research is showing the advisability of thinking and planning along K-12, K-college, and K-Ph.D. sequences.

The concept of a long-range English program seems to provide a more realistic sequencing of information and skills implicit in the discipline of English language art. Objectives are easier to see as partial, open-ended, nonterminal goals when a twenty or twenty-two year span is considered. By thinking along a K-Ph.D. sequence, the objectives of the various levels of English education come into sharper focus.

New Design is a series of recommendations to teachers at various educational levels. It asks that at whatever level English education is conducted, it explore the subject matters of four components: literature, public communication, language, and composition. It asks further that the daily lessons allow time for students to gain experience in practicing the language arts. It suggests that by integrating the eighteen components of the English discipline with one another, and by returning to these components year after year, the English teacher will, in the present, traditional time structure, have sufficient time to bring his students to an appropriate standard of literacy.

1

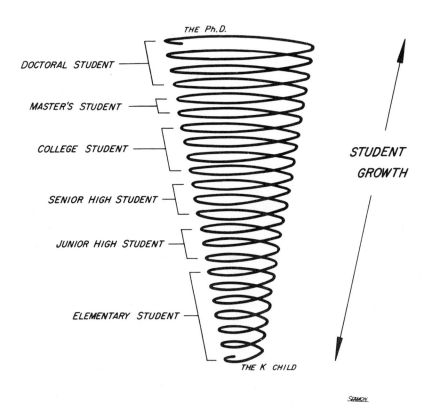

Figure 1. *The K-Ph.D. English curriculum design.*

THE KINDERGARTEN-DOCTORAL
ENGLISH CURRICULUM

Figure 1 shows the possibility of structuring a long-range English curriculum consisting of many components taught at successive educational levels. Such a planned program takes the form of an inverted cone-shaped spiral. The K-Ph.D. concept of English curriculum structure, though built on a twenty-two step chronological sequence (one academic year for each step), is not a rigid structure. The student himself, whether child or adult, is always at the rotating center of the curriculum, because the subject matter of English is adjusted to his needs by the classroom teacher. It is the student's capacity and competence that actually limit the amount of information and skill training he can receive at any given level. It is the curriculum designer's choice and the classroom teacher's ability that determine the peculiar mix of a semester's work or a day's lesson. The fundamental components of the English discipline, literature, communication, language, and composition, are introduced in miniature at the kindergarten level. (Figure 2 shows these major divisions.) In successive years, new information and skill training are added to each of the major components. Although the child is working through the same components as his Ph.D. father, he is at no time assumed to have the breadth of knowledge and competency which his father demonstrates.

One of the major advantages of a full-range English curriculum construct is its psychological validity. It encourages meaningful breadth and balance at every level of the planned school program. All students are expected to develop competency in the *total* English discipline. The problematic case of the fifth grade boy who reads at 12.8 grade level is readily solved. This student needs broadening experiences in a total English program at his grade level. Reading, even when considered a multiple skill, constitutes less than fifteen percent of the total English discipline. Similar dilemmas created for students on the level of doctoral specialization are also obviated by a K-Ph.D. curriculum. When enough K-18 broad-field experience in English education has been given to the doctoral candidate, his specialization is pursued with proper balance and perspective. The candidate's knowledge and skill gained from his eighteen years of composition, communication, linguistics, and literature not only maintain his specialization in perspective but also provide a reservoir for his postdoctoral teaching and research. New Ph.D.'s often work in areas of English far removed from their doctoral specialty.

Another advantage of a kindergarten-doctoral curriculum sequence is its administrative feasibility. It can be eased into any existing English education structure. Inservice education of teachers prepared to imple-

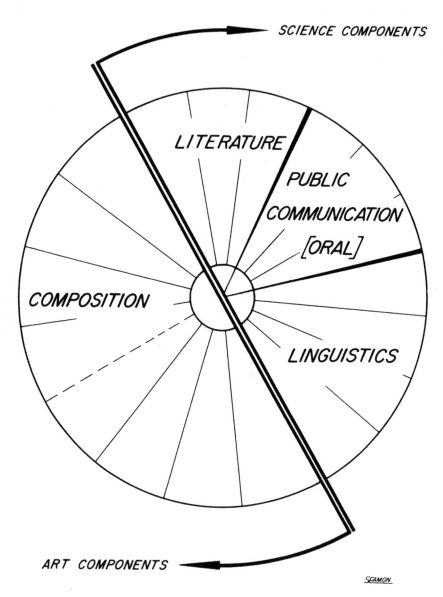

Figure 2.   *Major divisions of the English curriculum.*

ment a four component curriculum is minimal at the start. Once the concept is understood, the individual classroom teacher is responsible for providing a total English experience for the students in his charge. Existing courses of study for grade levels can be modified or developed through action research conducted by teachers in their regular daily work.

A MULTICOMPONENT ENGLISH CURRICULUM

Whether taught in kindergarten, elementary school, high school, college, or graduate school, a complete English curriculum includes four major components: language, literature, composition, and communication. Traditionally, English educators have been concerned about the tripod of language, literature, and composition; the power and universality of today's mass media, however, are difficult to ignore. Figure 3 shows the major divisions of a multicomponent English curriculum designed for instruction in English as a single grade level.

New Design recommends that English curriculums from kindergarten to graduate school coincide with the basic substructural pattern of the discipline itself.[1] Today the student needs a total English experience: this means information and skill training in a multicomponent discipline consisting of language, literature, composition, and communication. Although these four major components of English serve to identify the verbal products created by verbal artists in the discipline, a number of subcategories must be identified, if the *processes* or *methods* by which these verbal artifacts were created are to be transmitted to students in the discipline. Furthermore, research in the teaching of English is impossible unless the underlying components of the English discipline are carefully delineated.[2]

A close examination of Figure 3 shows that literature has three subdivisions: literary analysis, literary criticism, and literary history. Communication, identified specifically as *mass oral* has three subdivisions: public oratory, videotape media, and soundtape/disc media.[3] Language, or the broader term, linguistics, has four subdivisions: language coding/ decoding, language grammars, language history, and language geography. The process of reading, whether it involves nursery stories or Middle English ballads, is essentially an interpretation of graphic symbols; hence its inclusion in the major category of linguistics.

[1] A complete rationale for this statement is developed by the text.
[2] See N. L. Gage, ed., *Handbook of Research on Teaching* (Chicago: Rand McNally and Company, 1963).
[3] These divisions were cited as tentative by researchers. With feedback from its present test situation in the Abraham Lincoln clinical school construct (Washington, D.C.), *New Design* may recommend more astute subdivisions in its later revision.

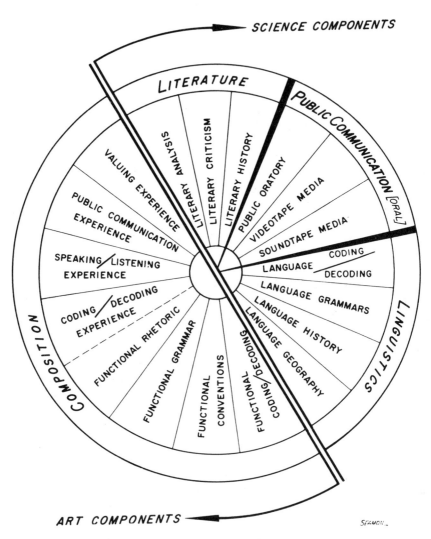

Figure 3. *The multicomponent English curriculum.*

Composition is, by far, the largest segment of a total English curriculum. The term is used in its broad sense of *putting together,* but the process is limited to the discipline of verbal art. Composition includes eight minor components, four related to functional instruction, and four related to performance.[4] Pre-performance information is categorized as functional coding/decoding,[5] functional conventions, functional grammar, and functional rhetoric. The four componets related to the students' overt performance in the English discipline include coding/decoding experience, speaking/listening experience,[6] public communication experience, and valuing experience.

These eighteen subject matter divisions constitute a modern English curriculum: three in literature, three in public communication, four in linquistics, and eight in composition.[7] Today the discipline called English has this interesting physiognomy; tomorrow the addition of new knowledge may well suggest another profile. In spite of the changes that will necessarily affect the components in the English discipline, it is not likely that the major substructure of the discipline will be altered. The long historical development of literature, linguistics, composition, and communication has firmly established the basic structural design of English. It will be another century when we can say that the English discipline has other than four major components.

FREEDOM AND DISCIPLINE

A distinctive characteristic of the academic discipline called English is that it encompasses two extremes of intention: on the one hand it encourages the freedom of the artist; on the other it imposes the disci-

---

[4] Throughout this text, the term *performance* should be construed as *action perceived externally.* For example, a child *performs* when he takes a statement of fact made by an informing agent (teacher, book, film, tape, and others), synthesizes it with other known information, and produces some verbal product.

[5] The author assumes that coding implies decoding, that is, that a person must be able to reconstruct a graphemic notation (encode) if he is to read it (decode). Reading, unless it is guesswork, presupposes writing.

[6] British educators use the term *oracy* to designate the speaking activity of students. It might be useful to use this term in English education research.

[7] These curriculum categories were revealed by action research projects of experienced English teachers enrolled in graduate courses at The Ohio State University and The University of Maryland. In structuring, teaching, and evaluating daily English lessons, teachers found that objectives and subject matter fell into identifiably distinct areas related to literature, language, composition, and communication.

In discussing teaching styles, these teachers found it useful to refer to specific subcategories of components rather than to one of the major divisions of the curriculum. The major divisions of the English discipline include subcategories which (because they are a result of different verbal methods of production) seem to require different teaching styles when transmitted to students. Subcategories are not absolute; consistency in naming them, however, seems to improve professional communication.

pline of the scientist.[8] An examination of the multicomponent English curriculum shows that ten of the components are identifiably sciencelike while eight are artlike. This means, of course, that the components demonstrate this distinction under the aspect of a teachable subject matter. The principle of integration fundamental to success in the teaching of English at any educational level is achieved by *meshing* the science and art components. Figure 4 illustrates the concept of two kinds of components working together to effect verbal competency in students. Practically speaking, the points of contact between those components related to science and those related to art need not be prestructured in curriculum designing at the level of school or whole year constructs; the classroom teacher engineers the meshing of components needed by students in a particular class.

A cursory analysis of the two major kinds of English curriculum components reveals a number of important facts about the subcomponents of the discipline. Literary analysis, literary criticism, and literary history are the subjects of a scientific inquiry which can be initiated in kindergarten and taught with increasing breadth at each of the twenty steps of a planned curriculum that ends only in graduate school. At this point journalism and drama, so long considered renegades to English departments, can be studied seriously as popular art and literary form respectively. Individual creative thinking will show how the very small child can begin his English education by learning not only how to recite nursery rhymes but also how to identify literary forms. Similarly, the upper elementary school child and the junior high pupil can learn, for example, the classifications of lyric poetry: ode, elegy, sonnet, song, and simple lyric; the characteristics of the form, the author's technique, the importance of a work's historical matrix, and the opinion of critics regarding the work.

As a subject of systematic inquiry, mass oral communication is rich in information. All the forms and methods of public address, both old and new, are interesting. The strengths and weaknesses of the various mass media challenge comparison at every age; the content of the media provides endless fascination and material for anlysis and comparison with other kinds of oral art products.

Linguistics, the scientific study of language which includes coding, language history, language geography, and language grammars, is also appropriately considered a subject for inventory, classification, and other learning experiences. Like mass oral communication and like literature, linguistics as a school subject deserves the rigor of teaching-learning methods and the exactness of objective evaluation required by all sci-

[8] Commission on English, *Freedom and Discipline* (New York: College Entrance Examination Board, 1965).

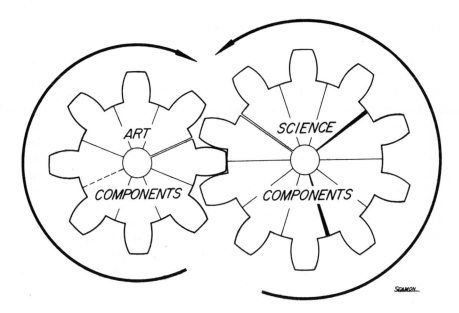

Figure 4. *The interaction of science and art components.*

ences. All four components of a complete English program provide information for the student which he needs to deepen his knowledge and understanding of the linguistic realities peculiar to his world. The information might be said to consist of *know-that* facts which, when presented systematically, help the child to achieve an orderly, true-to-fact comprehension of his verbal environment.

Composition, on the other hand, epitomizes the freedom implicit in verbal performance. Whereas the student *learning about* literature, communication, and linguistics is primarily concerned with factual information, the student *involved in* composition is directly confronted with the need to create. His study of coding/decoding, functional conventions, functional grammar, and functional rhetoric are directly related to the know-how skills he needs to perform verbally. His work, like all art production, must be personal; he himself is the center of his verbal creation. In his reading and writing excercises, in his speaking and listening exercises, in his public communication exercises, and in his valuing exercises, the child uses the principles of performance with the freedom of the verbal artist, which indeed he is.

In the discipline called English, the single integrating thread of the several components is the fact of *verbal interpretation of reality*. This means that all the subject matter of the English discipline, as it has defined itself historically and as we understand it today, consists of someone's verbal interpretation of reality. Whether the interpretation is direct as in the case of the novelist, or whether it is derived as in the case of the literary critic who interprets an interpretation, the work is always marked with the peculiar verbal physiognomy and creative power of its author. This quality of uniqueness, characteristic of all artistic production, makes verbal art necessarily a free and personal activity. The child who is taught to perceive the world around him and to interpret his perceptions verbally is being trained in the basic mode of the discipline called English. Freedom must characterize the teaching-learning aspects of composition if anything truly personal and unique is to be produced by students.

It seems that in the past the gravest error made by teachers was to confuse the *know-that* and *know-how* components in the English program; the science components were given the cursory treatment ordinarily reserved for principles of performance while the art components were evaluated with the rigor of a science. In a subject like English, consisting of four major components and eighteen subdivisions, it is important both to teach and to study according to the style suggested by the material involved. Instruction, whether at the kindergarten or graduate school level, should consciously preserve the balance between freedom and discipline so well sustained by the components themselves. Figure 5 shows

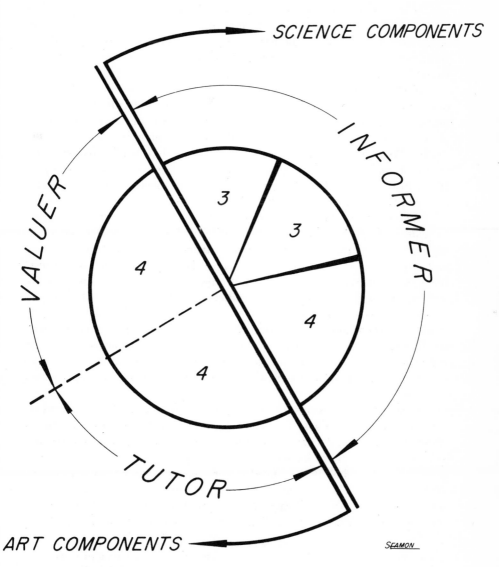

Figure 5. *Major teaching styles implicit in "New Design."*

three major teaching styles related to a curriculum consisting of *know-that* and *know-how* data.

When the teacher is concerned with the factual components in English and intends to transmit information *about* these realities,[9] he acts as an informant, using a didactic verbal style. When films, tapes, discs, computers, and other extensions of the teacher are used, the style of the chosen medium should match the teacher's.

When the teacher is concerned with functional *know-how* skills of students, he acts as a tutor. This means that he helps individuals use information in producing something. The goal of producing a verbal artifact of some kind motivates and guides the activity of both tutor and student.[10] This kind of instruction is personal and depends for its efficiency on the *know-how* experience of the teacher. There is no time lapse between instruction and trial creation; both go on together. The tutor tells how and the student tries out the instruction immediately.

When the teacher is concerned with the student's performance of *know-how* skills, he acts as a valuer. Having instructed and guided the student's trial verbal creations, he now structures a formal presentation and responds to the student's performance. His style here includes assessment or judgment, appreciation, and enjoyment.[11] When English activity requires a formal classroom audience, both teacher and students (those not performing) can share in the valuing experience. Furthermore, assessment and appreciation of students' verbal art can be a meaningful experience shared by teacher and students simultaneously in the classroom. Thus, three major teaching styles of informer, tutor, and valuer match the subcomponents of the multicomponent English curriculum.

In the didactic lessons, the teacher brings information to students in a variety of efficient ways. The student is expected to take in and understand the facts and concepts presented. The extent of his *intake* competency is checked by objective tests. In the practice lessons, the teacher gives *know-how* instruction needed for the creation of an immediate verbal product. The student is expected to synthesize the *know-how* information with his overall English conceptual framework and to produce some personal verbal creation. The extent of the student's skill is deter-

---

[9] These *know-that*, factual classes of information include literary analysis, literary history, literary criticism; public oratory, videotape media, soundtape media; language coding/decoding, language geography, language history, language grammars.

[10] These activities are designed to require *know-how* practice in functional coding/decoding, functional conventions, functional grammar, and functional rhetoric. The end products of the interaction of teacher and student is some verbal artifact which depends on the use of specific *know-how* skills.

[11] Components that require this teaching style include coding/decoding experience, speaking/listening experience, public communication experience, and valuing experience.

mined by the individual verbal product he creates. In the performance lessons, the teacher allows the student to perform verbally, responding in ways appropriate to a valuer (assessing, appreciating, enjoying). It is the category of *know-that* components that requires the *discipline* of scientific investigation; it is the category of *know-how* components, that requires the *freedom* of verbal art.

INTERRELATIONSHIPS IN THE
ENGLISH LANGUAGE ARTS

When the many components in the English program are carefully distinguished as *know-that* or *know-how* information, the problem of creating curriculums to suit diverse communities is simplified. Where children are poorly languaged,[12] it would seem reasonable to limit factual information about literature, public communication, and linguistics and to increase skill training information and practice. In no instance, however, at any educational level, can any one component be completely eliminated from the English education of the student. To teach a partial curriculum is to abort the linguistic development of the native speaker.

The four major components of the English curriculum, and their eighteen subdivisions as well, find their completeness and their educational value in the degree of their integration with one another. Whereas the amount of information in the science components can be limited for students requiring more functional, *know-how* work, the study of an entire component cannot be omitted. To present a partial curriculum is to present a false education in English. Any student, a culturally deprived one perhaps more than others, needs to know, for example, that his struggle to make meaning out of reality is shared by all men, especially verbal artists. He ought to realize that the principles he applies in making verbal interpretations of reality are the same principles in use for centuries by educated people. He has a right to be informed with the important common knowledge of all English educated persons—names of great writers, major forms of literature, examples of commonly known prose and poetry, the meaning and general method of literary criticism, the strengths and weaknesses of various public media of communication, the names and purposes of various grammars, the causes of language development and deviance. Not only has the student, despite his cultural status, a right to this information, he also has the right to know how these facts are directly related to the realities of his own verbal situation. The student learns the common facts about his discipline and their

[12] This term was first used by Alexander Frazier, The Ohio State University, to designate the student who lacks overall language facility.

unique meaning for himself when the interrelationships among all the language art components are taught. The student sees his own problem in its proper context only when he sees the whole of the discipline. Furthermore, his experience becomes significant only by reference to the larger reality of the world of verbal interpretation encompassed by the whole discipline of English.

A SELF-INTEGRATED ENGLISH CURRICULUM

It is reasonable to suppose that the teaching or transmitting of a discipline would follow the main structural lines of that discipline. A curriculum, the planned teaching-learning experiences related to a body of knowledge, molds itself upon the distinguishing structure of the related discipline. In English, the K-Ph.D. curriculum follows four major divisions of components. In implementing such a curriculum, then, the discipline gains increasing relevance as the student sees the structure of relatedness that unifies the entire construct. In English, the pattern of connections among the components can be called a self-integrated one. This means that the separate components borrow their method and content from one another to achieve their identity. In other words, any one component is contained in any other one, except in different proportion and combination. Thus, each of the eighteen components is a unique compound, but each has basic elements in common with all other components. Literary criticism, for example, has the substance of literature as its subject matter (an essay, perhaps); it uses the rhetoric of explication, the linquistic knowledge of encoding, the speaking voice of public oratory, and the functional *know-how* of speaking and writing conventions; it becomes an experience in written rhetoric and in aesthetic valuing; it shares the common interpretive mode of all language art, verbal interpretation; and it works in the medium common to all components of English, the English language.

For this reason the discipline called English can be called a self-integrated one. For the same reason, the teaching of the discipline becomes efficient as the integrative design of the discipline is emphasized. A teacher implementing an English curriculum at any educational level is wise to stress the interrelationships among the components by means of a teaching style and verbal behavior that match the substructure of the discipline itself. The K-Ph.D. curriculum structure is recursive not only because the same components are taught again and again at successive levels of meaning, but also because a teacher brings in *know-that* and *know-how* information and skill related to all the other English components in order to buttress the teaching of a concept or behavior in one specific area. Figure 6 shows the kind of recursiveness used to insure genuine learning.

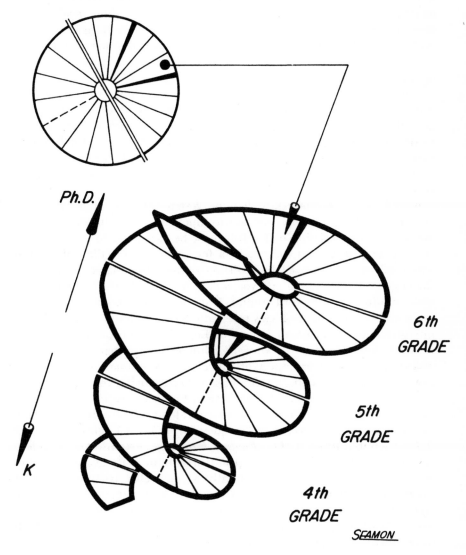

Figure 6.   *A recursive teaching method in K-Ph.D. English education.*

New Design suggests that students' problems be solved obliquely. This means, for example, that a student's reading rate deficiency be improved by speaking/listening experience, by public communication experience, by coding experience, as well as by decoding (reading) instruction, practice, and performance. By moving away from the specific problem and bringing the student in contact with the many-faceted discipline of English, the interrelationships of the multicomponents have an opportunity to work in the student's behalf.

A self-integrated program also means that teaching is limited to the subject matter of English. The eighteen components of the discipline (and their logical subdivisions) are integrated with one another and not with extraneous disciplines. Whatever is taught in the English curriculum must be justified by the following criterion: *Is the item in question about verbal art, about verbal art production, for an immediate verbal creation?*[13]

New Design recommends that the verbal behavior of both teacher and student be guided by the multicomponent curriculum content. In many cases, the teaching of English must be expanded to include more genuine *English* subject matter. In a few cases, the teaching of English will need to be improved by omitting non-English materials. It seems that a good many spelling and vocabulary words will need to be replaced with genuine English word studies. Lists of words related to foods, diseases, and general life problems take valuable curriculum time needed to intensify the self-integrated impact of English. Linguistic spelling rules, of course, are a part of the *know-that* linguistic information of coding/decoding, as well as an aspect of functional *know-how* language study.

The English teaching profession has been moving toward this kind of unified purposiveness in the teaching of English since 1956. Through a careful identification of the major structural lines of a curriculum, educators have tried to answer the key question, *What is English?* Although the 1956 publication of *The English Language Arts in the Secondary School* by the Commission on English Curriculum of the National Council of Teachers of English was hardly a comprehensive philosophy of English instruction, it was eminently useful. As a compendium of principles and experiences related to language arts for adolescents, it could be used by teachers to determine what specific emphases and purposes a high school program ought to have. By inference and deduction, objectives for English courses preceding and following levels 7-12 could be determined. The skills approach which this volume shared with its NCTE precedents,

[13] Graduate English interns at Trinity College, Washington, D.C., are presently testing the usefulness of this simple delimitation. Further restrictions may be necessary to specify increasingly *dense* levels of integration.

The English Language Arts and *Language Arts for Today's Children,* had the outstanding merit of emphasizing the fact that an English program ought to involve its participants as *persons practicing* the language arts.

In the last few years, however, national leadership expressed through such NCTE publications as *The National Interest and the Teaching of English, The National Interest and the Continuing Education of Teachers of English, The Preparation of Teachers of English,* and *The College Teaching of English* have created a new trend. The new direction is *away from* the former diversity and general experience-correlation heretofore applauded. The new emphasis is on structured sequence and academic integrity in the teaching of English as a discipline and the use of English in creative verbal behavior. Fortunately, proponents of the *new English* have been quick to develop relatively comprehensive rationales for the new curriculum designs. Based on the nature of the discipline and the needs of K-Ph.D. students, these programs, while different in many details, emerge with an identifiable unanimity of purpose. It is because the discipline of English has gradually taken shape that teacher training institutions can make realistic plans to prepare future teachers. Evidence of vital curriculum revision at the college level is given in the 1965 Tuttle survey of institutions with English education programs.

> The direction of planning clearly continues the trend indicated in the previous section toward greater specificity and away from free electives. . . . What has been facetiously described as "the smorgasbord major" seems to be on the way out.[14]

As the profession gradually refines its conceptual definition of a modern English curriculum, the more astute curriculum decisions can become and the better educated the English student can be. Curriculists,[15] especially those in the field of English, have been somewhat arbitrary in deciding what to teach and what to omit. As a common criterion for subject matter inclusion in the English curriculum is accepted, English teaching can maintain both its academic integrity and its relevance to students at every educational level and in any culturally divergent environment.

The self-integration concept presented by *New Design in the Teaching of English,* then, promotes a theory of *balance* which can be achieved by integrating the scientific components in the English discipline with the artistic. It suggests that students learn the methods and the facts that

---

[14] Donald R. Tuttle, *Curriculum Patterns in English* (Washington, D.C.: U. S. Government Printing Office, 1965), p. 49.

[15] A curriculist is a curriculum specialist. He does not develop curriculum theory, however; he builds curriculums for specific teaching situations.

verbal artists of distinction have used. It also suggests that students themselves make personal creative syntheses, using the content and the methods of English. *A self-integrated English curriculum means that the
subject matter of the teaching-learning situation is always within the con-
fines of the discipline.* There is continuous cross reference among the
eighteen components, so that throughout a twenty-two year period every
student can experience an identifiable English education. *New Design*
implies that English teaching is not the composite task of a total school or
university faculty; it is, rather, the unique task of the highly specialized
English educator.

THE PROBLEM OF METHODS

Few professional educators today clarify the difference between the
method of a discipline and the instructional method related to the teaching of a discipline. The difference in English is simply that disciplinary
method is the distinctive rhetorical mode by which verbal artists make
contributions to the accumulation of verbal artifacts. Instructional
method, however, is the pedagogical procedure through which the facts
and *know-how* of a discipline are transmitted from master to novice.
Methodology is the science of pedagogical procedure, and it is a science
old enough to know that each academic discipline has its unique instructional procedures.

To be sure, the success of an instructional procedure is directly related to the teacher's knowledge of subject matter and its inherent disci-
plining method. Unless a teacher can replicate the behaviors of verbal
artists, he can never teach these behaviors well. His success is related to
his mastery. This is not to say, however, that personal involvement in the
discipline is the *only* measure of teaching success. This may have been
true during the Renaissance, but it is hardly true today. The consum-
mate artist giving private lessons to his carefully selected pupil is not
ordinarily the pattern of modern education. Teachers today, whether
immersed in their discipline or not, are confronted with vast numbers of
nonselected pupils, many of whom have neither the talent nor the desire
to learn the subject at hand. Besides knowing his subject, the modern
high school teacher must have a precise knowledge of the psychology of
learning and of methods of large group instruction.

The teaching of English, then, follows methods related to the subject
matter of an eighteen component discipline. When the subject matter of
the science components can be used in genuine verbal creation, a high
level integration has been effected.

INSTRUCTIONAL METHODS IN ENGLISH

Few teachers today are skilled instructors by reason of having taken courses in methods in their professional training.[16] Most English teachers learn by classroom practice related to such general teaching methods as the Socratic, the rhetorical (associated with Aristotle, Cicero, and Quintilian), the Thomistic, the Montessori, the Herbartian, the Dewey method, and others.[17] There is no systematic teaching methodology in English and no special methods in English education available today. A recent emphasis on research in the teaching of English has not yet produced widely tested instructional methods.[18]

Teaching and using English methods means concern for an entire teaching process. In terms of *New Design,* it means meshing the science and art components of the English discipline so that they have genuine meaning for students at kindergarten-university levels. The value of the daily lesson structuring the implementation of this ideal must not be overlooked, because the teacher's own creative power is revealed by the conceptual strategies he develops in his daily lessons. *Creative daily lesson structuring is at the heart of teaching success in English.*

All teaching levels can be approached with two basic kinds of lesson plans, *procedural plans* and *formal plans. Procedural plans* are sequences of unrelated teaching-learning situations. To teach within the basic unit of a predetermined English period of 45 to 60 minutes, the teacher plans a variety of things the students will be doing in order to achieve certain stated objectives. Such a sequence of activities might include checking homework, doing an exercise in diagraming, taking a spelling quiz, and beginning the reading of an assigned short story. *Formal plans* are structures of teaching-learning situations, having formal identity and thematic unity. Such plans are models or paradigms of activity constructs planned for students during a given period. Each lesson has its own form and name and is identifiably different from other forms. The form of the lesson as well as its inner structure conveys a single, unified intention from teacher to student.

Whereas procedural plans are infinitely various, depending on the creative power and professional judgment of the teacher, formal plans, as

---

[16] National Council of Teachers of English, *The National Interest and the Continuing Education of Teachers of English* (Champaign, Illinois: National Council of Teachers of English, 1964).

[17] A useful source of information on general educational methods is Harry S. Broudy and John R. Palmer, *Exemplars of Teaching Method* (Chicago: Rand McNally and Company, 1965).

[18] The National Council of Teachers of English has recently (Spring, 1966) initiated a new journal emphasizing a scientific investigation of English methods, *Research in the Teaching of English.*

far as research has presently revealed, are limited to ten different kinds. Although fundamentally *prestructured,* as far as form is concerned, the formal lesson, like the procedural, depends upon the creative detail and astute judgment supplied by the individual teacher. In the last analysis, all lesson planning is highly creative. It is singularly artistic in that the teacher is responsible for each minute decision regarding what to teach, how to control interaction, how to sequence activities, how to evaluate learning, and how to effect a day-to-day continuum. Perhaps more than the procedural plan, the formal lesson structure challenges personal creativity. Not only must the teacher recreate his subject matter in terms of the formal structure he has chosen, but he must also create thematic coherence for his lesson. Since there are only ten formal structures, there is continuous pressure on the teacher to devise different sequential patterns of lessons and to apply these astutely to the teaching-learning realities of his classroom.

When to use procedural plans and when to use formal structures is often enigmatic, even to the experienced English teacher. The problem derives from the fact that teaching is an art dependent on a science, the science of human growth and development.[19]

At all levels of English education, students need a variety of structures to maintain high level interest and to benefit from a multicomponent discipline. Even college classes appreciate an occasional day when the instructor *finishes up* an assortment of classroom tasks such as going over an exam, checking in a project, planning a paper, and similar procedural activities. Exceptional students at either end of the ability span deserve some variety in structure. Repeated procedures tend to become monotonous, and students need the stimulus of the new and the challenging. The alert teacher structures his plans to fit the needs of his students, and whether his lessons are procedural or formal, he uses these structures to implement a discipline which is both a science and an art.

FORMAL STRUCTURES IN THE
TEACHING OF ENGLISH

Because English consists of multiple *know-that* and *know-how* components, experienced teachers tend to use certain formal structures for teaching the science components and others for teaching the art components. Of the ten kinds of formal lesson structures, eight seem best related to the *know-that* components and two seem most effective in teaching the *know-how* elements. The *science lessons* include the development lesson, the review, the drill, the test, the individual research lesson, the group

---

[19] An interesting discussion on the relationship of lesson structure to the intellectual level of students is initiated in Jack R. Frymier, *The Nature of Educational Method* (Columbus, Ohio: Charles E. Merrill Books, Inc., 1965), p. 206.

research lesson, the guided reading lesson (for difficult material), and the independent study lesson. The *art lessons* include the practice lesson and the performance lessons (discussion, enrichment, culmination).

All ten formal lessons as well as occasional procedural plans are needed to implement and integrate a multicomponent English curriculum in the secondary school. Each lesson structure implies that certain objectives can be achieved more efficiently through this structure than through another. The main principle of distinction among the formal structures is *not* the nature of the behavioral objective, whether cognitive, effective, or motor, but rather the nature of the hypothesized teaching-learning situation in terms of teacher behavior. In other words, the formal structures are distinguished from one another primarily by *what is going on* in the classroom from the teacher's point of view. It can easily be seen that the same structured activity might be used to achieve an unlimited number of different behavioral objectives in terms of student learning. In the eight lessons related to the *know-that* components (the science lessons), the students are engaged in learning factual material about literary analysis, literary history, literary criticism, public communication, language history, language geography, and language grammars.[20] In the two kinds of lessons related to the *know-how* components (the art lessons), the students are learning information which they need to compose verbal interpretations of reality, and they are busy composing.[21]

In relation to major teaching styles, the following lessons are associated with an informing style: the development, review, drill, test, individual research, group research, guided reading, and independent study lessons. The practice lesson is related directly to the tutorial style. The performance lessons are associated with the valuing style. Figure 7 shows the relationship of these lesson strategies to basic teaching styles.

Although the ten formal lesson structures are distinct by reason of what the teacher is doing, these structures have several procedural similarities. A cursory analysis of the outlines of these structures reveals these similarities.

STRUCTURES RELATED TO KNOW-THAT MATERIAL
(Informing Style)

DEVELOPMENT LESSON
 1. Lead
 2. Presentation
 3. Explanation
 4. Summary and evaluative remarks

[20] Refer to Figure 2.
[21] This classification of formal lesson plans is being tested at Abraham Lincoln School by the English interns of Trinity College, Washington, D.C., to check the validity and usefulness of the distinctions among formal lesson structures.

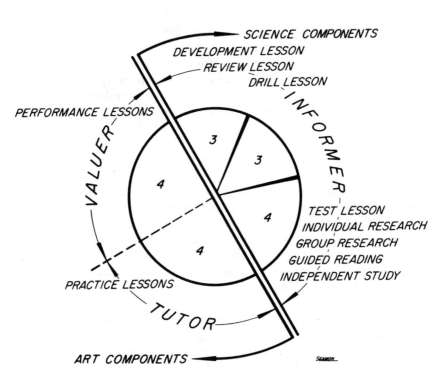

Figure 7.   *Formal lesson strategies implicit in "New Design."*

REVIEW LESSON
1. Lead
2. Presentation of oral or written questions
3. Quiz
4. Summary and evaluative remarks

DRILL LESSON
1. Lead
2. Statement of objective
3. Outline of procedure
4. Use of materials
5. Oral or written evaluation

TEST LESSON
1. Lead
2. Directions
3. Use of test device
4. Oral or written check-up

INDIVIDUAL RESEARCH LESSON
1. Lead
2. Presentation of questions or problems to individuals
3. Individuals go to work
4. Evaluative remarks

GROUP RESEARCH LESSON
1. Lead
2. Division into groups
3. Presentation of questions or problems to groups
4. Groups go to work
5. Evaluative remarks

GUIDED READING LESSON (for difficult material)
1. Lead
2. Presentation of topic to be covered
3. Oral questions (teacher waits until students find answer in text; they read it)
4. Summary and evaluation

INDEPENDENT STUDY LESSON
1. Lead
2. Statement of work to be done by entire class
3. Specific directions
4. Class goes to work
5. Oral or written evaluation

STRUCTURES RELATED TO KNOW-HOW MATERIAL
(Tutoring and Valuing Styles)

PRACTICE LESSON
1. Statement of skills

2. Practice of skills
3. Evaluation

PERFORMANCE LESSONS
Discussion Lesson
1. Statement of technique to be used (implies preteaching technique)
2. Statement of material to be discussed
3. Discussion
4. Evaluation and response
Enrichment Lesson (for use with pupil presentations)
1. Statement of topic
2. Presentation of verbal art product
3. Teacher summary
4. Group evaluation and response
Culmination Lesson
1. Statement of procedure
2. Student presentation of planned program
3. Evaluation by teacher and/or audience

It can be seen that the similarities in the lessons organized to teach *know-that* information include a lead, presentation of work to be accomplished, and some kind of summary or evaluation. In the lessons organized to teach *know-how* information the first point omits the lead, beginning instead with a statement of what is to be done, that is, the identification of a verbal artifact to be produced. In these lessons related to artistic components, the extensive personal involvement of the student in the lesson and the enjoyment ordinarily associated with the humanistic side of English seem to eliminate the necessity for the carefully devised motivational lead. It should be noted that in each of the ten kinds of formal lesson structures, provision is made for evaluation of some sort. Whether written or oral, detailed or cursory, student initiated or teacher directed, evaluation represents the reaction of people involved in the teaching-learning situation; it invests both the scientific and artistic components in the English curriculum with the qualities of humanistic endeavor; it unites teacher and student in a common response to a shared educational experience. Perhaps the similarities and differences of the ten formal lesson procedures vital to the implementation of a hybrid discipline like English will be clarified with a brief description of each lesson.

THE DEVELOPMENT LESSON

The purpose of the development lesson is to lead students to the acquisition of new and enriched knowledge. This particular type of information gathering lesson is used when the nature of the material, its difficulty, and the ability of the group make it impossible for the students to comprehend the essential ideas by reading independently.

Despite the amount of teacher activity that this lesson demands, it should not be interpreted as one in which the teacher does all the talking and thinking. On the contrary, through thought-provoking questions, he should stimulate his students to think and to recall all that they might already know about the topic. The minds of the students must be active during the entire period. This mental activity can be obtained by referring the students to the text to study pictures or charts, by directing them to read a sentence or paragraph to clarify and enrich a point just explained, or by using a variety of the audio-visual devices available today, such as the overhead projector, tape recorder, film strip projector, and others.

The lower the grade level and the ability of the group, the more frequently should the teacher use the development procedure. Occasionally, if the nature of the material warrants it, the development lesson can become mainly a demonstration in which the teacher shows the development of some process or movement. Ordinarily, however, in the language arts, demonstration is implicit in development and does not require an entire period of instruction. Often the development lesson is an enrichment lesson in which the teacher uses a variety of media to develop the students' cognitive/affective experiences.

THE REVIEW LESSON

In effective teaching, the review lesson is intended primarily to deal with material already covered. Usually it follows a development lesson or several such lessons. Often it comes at the end of a unit before the enrichment and culmination lessons.

Although the review lesson is based on material previously learned, it should reapply and expand the material presented so that students have an opportunity to reinforce their learning. The technique most often used in the review is oral questioning. Great care should be taken in the selection of particular questions so that they elicit pivotal concepts rather than irrelevant detail. A written review consisting of several key thought questions or a short quiz on important facts is especially effective when evaluated immediately in the classroom.

A review lesson constitutes an entire teaching period and has its own formal procedure. It should not be confused with *reviewing* which, as an aspect of summarization, occurs after most kinds of explanation or demonstration.

THE DRILL LESSON

The main objective of the drill lesson is to establish automatic, correct responses. Differing from the mixed practice lesson, the drill requires immediate simple responses, usually oral. Its distinguishing characteristic is speed.

Because effective drills are short, a drill lesson usually consists of several varied devices exercising the students in quick recall, identification, and similar cognitive skills. These lessons are most effective at the end of a unit of work, immediately preceding the test lesson. The best drills provide maximum participation for each student and often take the form of games. The number and frequency of the drill periods are determined by the needs of the group and by the type of material involved.

THE TEST LESSON

Although the test lesson is usually considered to be a means of measuring student ability, and, therefore, a means of evaluation for the teacher, this lesson also serves as a unique learning experience for the student. Every effort should be made, in spite of the student's performance, to keep the tone of the lesson positive and encouraging. Since tests are ordinarily used to check the accuracy of learning of the scientific components of the English curriculum, they should reflect the rigor of scientific measurement. For this reason, a test should come only after a sequence of other formal lessons which have thoroughly taught, enriched, reviewed, drilled, and applied the material at hand.

THE INDIVIDUAL RESEARCH LESSON

If sufficient materials can be brought into the classroom, this lesson can take place in the ordinary locale; otherwise it implies use of the library or other community resources. Structured for a single class period, or at most two periods, this lesson requires a different research task from each student. Most effective when carefully prestructured by the teacher, this lesson, like the group research, works well when the students are given discussion periods to report to the class. Students will often use a variety of media: tapes, photocopies, charts, chalk-diagrams, and others, to present their research report if they are allowed sufficient preparation time. A weekend or several school evenings is usually ample time. An ordinary written report can be done overnight.

THE GROUP RESEARCH LESSON

The classroom or library where groups of students work on common problems will necessarily be characterized by movement. Although separate groups may have a stockpile of materials relevant to their assigned task, individual members will move about, locating and sharing materials. Subdued conversation among members of a group is often necessary to achieve a task usually limited to one period's work.

When necessary, two or three days may be given to a sequence of research lessons. Experienced teachers, however, have noted that energy is frequently dissipated when long periods of time are allowed. Furthermore, multiple research periods imply mulitple discussion lessons, and these become monotonous to students if extended beyond two or three days.

Considerable structuring strategy is required of the teacher planning group research lessons. The astute selection of persons for each group as well as an assignment which fits the needs and interests of each group must be given attention. Often in the sixth or seventh grade, group leaders and recorders can be made responsible for dividing a problem among the various members of the group. Depending on the needs of the situation, the teacher can plan subsequent discussion periods in which either individual or group reports are given to the class.

THE GUIDED READING LESSON

Although slow students can be asked to do simple group and individual research tasks, they often need guided reading lessons to insure their comprehension of material before they work alone. This lesson involves bit by bit reading of a selection. Tne motivational leads and questions are supplied one at a time by the teacher; students read and respond. Especially suited to the reading of difficult poetry such as selections from Milton and T. S. Eliot, this lesson provides ample opportunity for the teacher to encourage, assist, and even cajole students through formidable written material. Sometimes called *combing,* this kind of lesson, when not required by the difficulty of the material, can become the master timewaster of the whole English program.

THE INDEPENDENT STUDY LESSON

Quiet, reflective independent work in the classroom under the supervision of the teacher marks the independent study lesson. Ordinarily all students use the same materials, each one at his own desk. Problems, questions, or objectives have been prestructured by the teacher, and the work must be completed by the end of the period. Usually the teacher provides a discussion lesson the following day when students can share their answers, solutions, and achievements with other members of the class. Many teachers collect the work in order to note the study efficiency of individual students. They return the papers the following day before proceeding with the discussion.

THE PRACTICE LESSON

Like the discussion lesson, this formal procedure is another major key to the *know-how* elements of the English curriculum. It allows the student to put his interpretations of reality into verbal form. Like the discussion lesson, the practice lesson is a vehicle of integration between the science and art components of a curriculum. What the drill is to scientific fact, the practice is to artistic production. Some practice lessons might be exercises in using each of the various modes of writing. Other lessons might be periods when the student tries to develop paragraphs by a variety of methods. Another might be the student's trying to do a sample of literary criticism. Another, writing sentences from formulas, or writing free verse.

The practice lesson should always begin and end in one period. Since it involves the student's *know-how* technique, it should be a pleasant activity rather than a tedious one. It should not be evaluated with the rigor of a test or drill lesson which belong to the scientific components rather than the artistic.

The mixed practice lesson includes a statement of the skills to be practiced, a period of practicing, and an evaluation. The purpose of this kind of lesson is to clarify or emphasize certain skills or to consolidate skills. The benefits of the lesson are threefold. First, the practice leads to overlearning which in turn leads to automatic or habitual response. Second, the practice increases the student's ability in a particular skill because he does the task differently each time he practices it. And third, the practice increases the student's understanding of the skills involved and the facts of the content used.

Despite these benefits, however, the practice lesson must be used with care. Most important, the student must know exactly what he is to do and how to do it. The practice lesson is not so much a time to introduce new learning as it is a time to review (practice) former learning. Care must also be taken to see that the practice is done in as comfortable a setting as possible. The period of practice should include variety and novelty. If drudgery or boredom set in, the practice period should be altered or suspended.

One of the most important parts of a practice lesson is motivation. If a student does not understand the purpose of the practice or if for some other reason he is not motivated, then much of the practice will be meaningless to him. There are several techniques for good motivation in practice. Genuine appreciation of effort is usually effective. Perhaps the best motivation, however, is the self-motivation of students themselves. This is often the result of the student seeing his own weaknesses and charting his own improvement. Self-diagnosis and self-direction, then, are important in the various practice lessons.

In addition to the content and the motivation of a practice lesson, the teacher has the responsibility to supervise the practice carefully. It is especially important that the teacher watch closely to make failure impossible at the outset. He should continue to watch that the student's practice is *correct* practice. Often a little consultation prevents errors.

In many instances a practice lesson is followed by a discussion lesson in which students can share their successful writing productions with others. Groups hearing and examining the members' work often provide sufficient evaluation and appreciation. Sometimes the teacher can grade the papers and display them on the bulletin board. This practice, however, becomes futile when several days are allowed to lapse between the practice and the evaluation and when a limited number of the same papers are repeatedly chosen for display.

PERFORMANCE LESSONS

The Discussion Lesson. This lesson is one of the major keys to the performance *know-how* components of the English curriculum. It provides the student with the means of expressing orally his verbal interpretations of reality. Because a worthwhile speaking presupposes serious *composing* activity, discussion at any educational level best meets English objectives when it is *structured* rather than *free*. A planned discussion lesson uses an identifiable discussion technique which the students have been taught to use in a previous development lesson. These techniques have the outstanding merit of impelling the student to *deliberate* and *compose* his ideas before presenting them. Eight efficient discussion techniques especially suited to an integrated high school English curriculum follow.

A. *Informal Group Discussion.* In the classroom, the entire class may be used; in committee situations, fifteen should be the maximum number. Smaller numbers are more efficient.

The entire class prepares answer to a set of specific questions. The point is *to shade* the answers with valuable personal experience so that 10 or 12 varied and rich answers may be given to the same question. The chairman asks the questions after giving a reasonably long introduction of the type of material to be discussed. Students may answer spontaneously by rising and addressing the chairman.

B. *Informal Panel Discussion.* In the classroom, six or seven students is a good number of participants. The *agenda* consists of definite questions previously given by the teacher and prepared by the students. The questions are of such a nature as to allow for a multiplicity of response.

The chairman should be a capable student. His duties are as follows:

1. He introduces at some length the topic to be discussed.
2. He introduces by name the members of the panel, adding, "and myself, Jim Smith".
3. After the discussion he throws the panel open to the floor and asks for critical evaluation.

The chairs for a panel should be arranged so that the members see one another. A semicircle is best for the classroom. The chairman is seated in the center. Experienced teachers have found that when each speaker *rises* for his contribution, he communicates more effectively.

C. *Symposium.* As many as eight students may participate. Each speaker presents (reads) a paper on one phase of the topic under discussion. Each is introduced individually before reading his paper. He acknowledges the introduction by saying, "Thank you," and adding the chairman's name.

The chairman's duties are as follows:

1. Introduces the topic.
2. Introduces each speaker and the title of his paper.
3. Gives a brief summary of the reports and a concluding talk.
4. Asks for contributions, evaluations, and criticisms from the floor.

D. *Discussion 66.* The class is divided into groups of six. Each group selects its own leader who acts as secretary. The work of each group is to formulate answers to specific questions or problems assigned by the teacher. These may be the same for all groups or different, according to the discretion of the teacher. Sufficient time must be allowed for each student to formulate his answers. Then each contributes his material orally to the group of which he is a member.

When all groups have found solutions to their problems, the teacher calls the leaders to the front of the class to present the compilations of each group. The teacher then summarizes the work of the period and makes a few concluding remarks.

E. *Debate* (informal classroom procedure). Whether formal or informal, debate is defined as oral controversy, or intellectual argument. Because of this, the success of any debate depends upon the specific and careful preparation of the participants.

In the classroom, three speakers on the affirmative side and three on the negative are usually enough. The procedure is as follows:

1. Chairman (not one of the debaters) introduces the general topic which the class has been working on.
2. Chairman introduces the *debate question,* linking it with the general topic.
3. Chairman introduces the speakers, affirmative side first.
4. He opens the period of rebuttal.

5. He closes the period of rebuttal and calls for the decision of the judges.

Points to note:

1. Ordinarily, the chairman introduces each speaker immediately before he is to give his debate talk. For classroom efficiency, however, this can be done all at once.

2. In a formal debate the speakers take a turn, beginning with the first speaker on the negative side, in presenting their rebuttal speech. In the classroom, however, an open rebuttal period is more satisfactory. The time allowed for the rebuttal is previously determined by the teacher and announced by the chairman. Three minutes is usually sufficient in grades 7-12. College students can sustain worthwhile argument for as long as ten minutes, depending on the quality of English students in the class.

3. Students must prepare diligently in the research lesson preceding the debate, if they are to experience the multiple values of this kind of English discussion. Significant values include the following: (a) satisfies an innate love of argument; (b) develops sportsmanship; (c) vitalizes classroom routine; (d) stimulates and clarifies thought; (e) offers speech experience to many students; (f) trains students to consider multiple views on a question before reaching decisions.

F. *Dialogue.* Two persons converse with one another, developing a major, identifiable idea. Often the dialogue becomes an *interview* in which one speaker questions and the other responds. The Socratic dialogue is often effective in the hands of an intelligent pair of students.

G. *Dialogue Forum.* Two persons presenting a dialogue may choose to invite audience reaction or participation. Members of the class may respond freely.

H. *Reports* (group or individual presentations). Sharing information a student has discovered becomes most effective when the group becomes involved with the ideas presented through questions and comments. Evaluation, except for a brief remark, is probably secondary to what the student is trying to communicate. Many reports are vitiated by an emphasis on evaluation rather than communication. As a discussion technique, reporting is assumed to stimulate audience response. The wise teacher does not interfere in any of the discussion procedures once the students have initiated them; instead, he goes to the rear of the room and enjoys them for as much as they are worth. Since what the students are doing represents an artistic verbal achievement, the teacher should refrain from negative, critical comments.

The Enrichment Lesson. The enrichment lesson presents material which deepens or extends the subject under consideration. Often it is used to intensify the student's understanding and appreciation of values. Because many high school students have limited experience with verbal art forms, enrichment can be provided by students interpreting Shakespeare films, theater trips, museum visits, filmstrips, recordings of famous speeches, poems, and dramas, and similar experiences. Students themselves provide the best enrichment experiences for others in the class when they read original poems, enact skits and plays, illustrate ideas from literature pictorially, and give reports on research or personal experience related to the subject.

Group response and evaluation is important in enrichment lessons because it encourages sincere valuing behavior in response to artistic production. Verbal comment from members of the class is often enough; occasionally a written reaction is desirable.

The Culmination Lesson. Just as the culminating point of a lesson is its highest peak of achievement, so the culmination of a unit is its period of greatest importance. This lesson is an opportunity for students to draw together the knowledge, skills, and insights from a particular unit of study into a creative personal synthesis. The importance of the culmination is that students produce it. It might be a display of books with living authors reporting; it might be the run-off in a poetry contest; it might be a series of reports on some phase of the unit; it might be a contest or an auditorium program. Whatever the nature of the culmination, preparation for it should generate genuine enthusiasm. Furthermore, it ought to involve both the science components of the curriculum and the art components. In every instance it should be a fitting and memorable formal experience in verbal art for the students.

In the last analysis, the implementation of a multicomponent, self-integrated English curriculum at any K-Ph.D. level depends on the strategy of daily lesson structuring. In the hands of the teacher rests the reality of whether a curriculum will help a student to function creatively in verbal art or whether that curriculum will enervate his verbal creativity. Whether a teaching method at any kindergarten-university level is procedural or formal is not the crucial problem. The problem is, instead, whether or not a teacher can structure and sequence daily English lessons to effect a synthesis between the scientific *know-that* information of the curriculum and the student's need to use this information in improving his own verbal behavior.

II

Composition, Creativity, and Language Arts Instruction

Composition is central to the teaching of English. Both instruction and performance in composition can be creative if the teacher and student appreciate the fundamental difference between the science and art components in the English discipline, and if teaching and learning styles relate to these differences without effacing the basic unity of all language art.

THE GENERATING PROCESS

There can be no valid instruction in language art if the method ignores the fact that composing is the process underlying every component in the English discipline. Nothing can be expressed in oral or written form unless it is first composed. In the discipline called English, there is always a human agent giving personal expression to some reality. The expression comes under the aegis of the discipline when the generation is communicative and verbal. The quality of communicability presupposes orderly arrangement on the part of the agent. There are no elaborate rules for orderliness in verbal human communication: only one, intelligibility. The gammar and rhetoric of a language provide a system that guarantees intelligibility in the generating process.

Whenever a person organizes his perceptions of reality and gives them verbal expression, he is *composing* in the best sense of the word. Composition is the foundational process in a discipline committed to excellence in verbal interpretation of reality. Thus, literature is composition; literary criticism is composition; literary history is composition; articles on language history, geography, and linguistic theory are composition; speech presupposes composition; a knowledge of grammar, rhetoric, and the conventions of writing is implicit in composition. None of the eighteen components in the English discipline, therefore, can be understood apart from its reality as a product of a generative composing act.

Of course, it can be argued that composition in this broad sense of *process* underlies every discipline, being synonymous with life itself. This is true, certainly, because all living things by interaction with their environment are involved instinctively, consciously, or both in a dynamic compositional process.

LANGUAGE ARTS INSTRUCTION

The fact that the process of composition replicates a fundamental life process is relevant to instructional theory in English where the fundamental aim is to teach the child the information and skills he needs to make meaning out of reality. By giving composition the emphasis it merits in the English curriculum, the school helps the child to interact in a verbally efficient way with his environment, not only perceiving it in a passive, nonverbal way, but influencing, creating, and shaping it by his compositional linguistic power. Ultimately the child who achieves satisfactory composition skill finds delight in creative verbal production. Not only does a writer grow in creativity by producing language products, but the writer also defines himself by means of the compositional process.

Whether language arts instruction is given in elementary school or graduate school, one fact is clear: verbal interpretation is the mode (*modus operandi*) of the English discipline. Any instruction, therefore, must include both the *know-that* and *know-how* aspects of verbal interpretation. Teaching has been only partially accomplished when the student knows *about* an English component. He must be able to use his information in a personal creative way if it is to have any genuine meaning for him. In English it is assumed that the mode of creative behavior will be a verbal one appropriate to the informational content. In the case of young children or disadvantaged students with a limited verbal repertory, it is necessary to encourage the composing process through such modes as musical expression, bodily movement, pictorial representation, and other means. At the same time, however, the students' experience in hearing a variety of *verbal* interpretations must be extended. For this purpose, appropriate songs, poems, recitations, dramatizations, and stories should be presented orally to the children to improve their ability to perceive, understand, and respond to a variety of linguistic interpretations of reality. The teacher needs to exercise good judgment in deciding when an individual student or small group will profit most from a listening activity, and when active participation seems warranted.

THE PROBLEM OF EXCELLENCE

Few students enter high school with a wide experience in recognition and use of the many compositional forms included in the English heritage. It is easy for educators to understand, then, why students find it impossible to be *creative* in English. A lack of knowledge and experience in using the verbal art forms traditional in English handicaps verbal expression and makes it difficult to achieve any measure of personal satisfaction in one's verbal interpretations. It limits the student to a few undifferentiated structures such as a story, a poem, a theme, or a paragraph. No matter how well a student understands that composition is the unifying structure of the language arts and that verbal interpretation is its mode, he must have definite examples (forms) of literary art if he is to achieve anything worthwhile in creative personal interpretation of reality.

Generally speaking, a student's verbal art is *worthwhile* if it meets two standards: the individual's need to feel pleasure in his creation, and the objective criteria traditionally applied to separate literary forms. Evaluation is defeated when students are not familiar with the body of long-distinguished literary forms in the English discipline. Factitious evaluation becomes more disastrous for the student than it does for the teacher. When the student has no objective criteria by which to measure the validity and effectiveness of his verbal interpretations, the subjective appreciation of his own art is minimized. The younger the student, the less able he is to produce work from which he receives a minimum of delight. The younger the student, the more he needs the support of structure.

One disservice the elementary teacher can do the children is to neglect the teaching of formal structure. In an effort to make composition easy a teacher asks children to write or tell about some subject, instead of asking them to create a form. Much more is accomplished when every request specifies both form and content. For example, the teacher might say to a fourth grade class, "let's write a ballad about a lumberjack lost in a forest," or to a first grade group, "Listen to this dialogue between Red Ridinghood and the wolf." Evaluation then is conducted in terms of the form as well as the content. Did the fourth graders indeed produce a ballad? What made their verbal creation this form of narrative poetry rather than a metrical tale? Did the first graders hear the dialogue between the little girl and the wolf? What did the wolf say? What did Red Ridinghood answer?

Unless literary forms are introduced in the early years of school, children are deprived of a number of things: factual information about the various forms; skill in distinguishing one form from another; experience in verbal interpretation through a variety of forms; satisfaction from meeting objective structural requirements of many verbal forms. Unless children begin using a variety of forms in the elementary school, it is difficult to achieve language facility in both speech and writing by the time they are finished with high school. Furthermore, habits of careless work resulting from poorly motivated effort are difficult to supplant with enthusiasm and creative verve in high school and college English courses.

Since verbal interpretation of distinction has form, it will be difficult, if not impossible, for high school students to achieve excellence in their verbal interpretations without experience in handling various art forms. T. S. Eliot's maxim, that literature "should entertain, teach wisdom, and be an example of an art form," is good advice at any level of language arts instruction.[1] The student learns the requirements of particular verbal art forms by working with them. There are far too many forms to analyze, appreciate, and reproduce in four or five years of secondary education. Then too, the English major who begins his specialization in the discipline must understand the relationship of his specialty to other forms in the discipline if he is to understand it correctly.

Conscious of the concepts of literary forms, a student not only delimits and focuses his own writing, he also learns to perceive form in all verbal interpretations and to identify the structural relationships of form to verbal distinction. One reason students fail to achieve their potential as writers might well be the fact that they are kept on the *write about* exercises their whole academic life. Paragraphs are not verbal art forms, regardless of their subject matter. They are building units, and they have a limited value apart from a larger rhetorical construct. Neither are themes art forms, though the classical rhetoricians used them to exercise students in keeping to a central idea when writing. Themes were a developmental step in the teaching of writing: they were intended to be end products of creative verbal effort. At best they can ill-serve this end, lacking the true distinction of an art form. Because very young children can compose fables, anecdotes, lyric poetry, short plays, and other verbal art forms with confidence and success, there is little reason for the stalemate on themes and paragraphs in the elementary school, the high school, or in freshman composition courses.

THE PROBLEM OF INTEGRATION

An integrated English curriculum at any instructional level requires that students compose, as far as possible, in the literary forms which are generally accepted as belonging to the discipline which they study. When

---

[1] T. S. Eliot in Thomas Baily, "The Dynamic Future," *National Association of Secondary School Principals Bulletin,* Vol. 48 (March, 1962), p. 162.

students are asked to *write about* things, they are often at a loss as to what form is appropriate to their subject and what techniques will facilitate their expression of ideas. Teachers can help students write well by suggesting appropriate forms for compositions as well as by suggesting challenging content. Rather than directing a student to write about his summer vacation, for example, the teacher might ask him to write an informal essay, a newspaper editorial, or a satire on some aspect of this subject. Such a challenge motivates the student to learn what constitutes the various literary and rhetorical forms. It also provides the teacher with the opportunity of turning the *know-that* information of literary analysis into a demostration of *know-how* compositional skill.

Efficiency of instruction suggests that composing in a particular form should immediately follow the analysis and appreciation of literary examples in that form. Thus the study of Helen Keller's autobiography suggests the creation of a personal autobiography; the analysis of Wordsworth's *England, 1802* suggests the creation of a sonnet.

Reproducing literary forms for the purpose of learning *about the form* is a sterile exercise at any level. Unless the teacher can find a reason related to the student's genuine needs, the ideal of integration is best left untouched. Writing for factitious, artificial reasons vitiates much of the verbal art in today's schools. Students will write well only when there is a *real* reason for writing well. True, research has shown that elementary children write better from *derived* experience than from direct experience. However, this means that the experience was one related to reading a book, watching a movie, and others.[2] It does not mean that the experience was *contrived*. Writing is too difficult to do well from extrinsic motives alone. Contrived reasons are rejected or accepted passively by students. It is this point of *phoniness* in English composition that school dropouts often cite as a cause of rebellion.

MOTIVATING COMPOSITION

Experienced teachers will admit that most oral activities in the English classroom succeed, whereas a good many writing activities fail. A fundamental reason for this fact is related to the motivation of composing activities. Oral activities usually succeed because the speaker is pressed by the exigencies of a real audience. Oral activities seem to suc-

---

[2] Perhaps confusion would be minimized if derived experience were classified and called *second level direct* experience. Reading a book about a horseback riding problem is, after all, as direct an experience as having the problem with a horse. The point is, however, that in the first case, the book (author) interprets the experience for the reader; in the second case, the reader must make his own verbal interpretation of the problem. Direct experience then is bilevel; *first level direct* and *second level direct* (erroneously called *derived*).

ceed best in high school where the adolescent is keenly sensitive to the responses of his peer audience.

In written composition it is difficult to achieve *real* motivation. There is the reality of writing letters to living authors, writing skits and plays to entertain other classes, writing invitations to school programs, producing newspapers, literary magazines, and yearbooks, and others. However, motivation for individual efforts related to a unit of literature takes considerable planning. Quintilian offers the following suggestions for motivating the writing efforts of the beginner.

> His studies must be made an amusement: he must be questioned and praised and taught to rejoice when he has done well; sometimes too when he refuses instruction, it should be given to some other to excite his envy, at times also he must be engaged in composition and should be allowed to believe himself successful more often than not.[3]

In a later book Quintilian discusses the motivational power intrinsic to the art of speaking itself.

> For the sheer necessity of speaking thrusts forward and forces out our laboring thought, and the desire to win approbation kindles and fosters our efforts. So true is it that there is nothing which does not look for some reward, that eloquence, despite the fact that its activity is in itself productive of a strong feeling of pleasure, is influenced by nothing so much as the immediate acquisition of praise and renown.[4]

Besides motivation and the need of the student for much writing and speaking experience, the classical writers often wrote on the subject of appropriate composition assignments. They were in agreement on the value of commonplace exercises, and believed that these discussions on general questions, such as the nature of injustice, served to exercise and develop a student's power to invent and arrange a speech. Neither Aristotle, Cicero, nor Quintilian, in affirming or disagreeing with contemporary opinions on the best topics to use for exercises, mentions the composing of sentences or paragraphs as an elementary exercise. Themes were not mentioned either, though theses, speeches affirming or denying certain generally used statements, were sometimes substituted for the commonplaces. The difference between the two exercises, as Cicero explains, was that the first demanded only clear exposition, whereas the second required the maintenance of a position and, consequently, argumentation. The debate speech was considered a simple exercise because, in Aristotle's terms, such a composition needed no proem and little narration. Quintilian recommended the paraphrasing of both prose and

---

[3] Quintilian, *Institutio Oratoria*, Vol. I (Books I-III), H. E. Butler, trans. (Cambridge, Massachusetts: Harvard University Press, 1959), p. 31.

[4] Quintilian, IV, *op. cit.*, p. 143.

poetry, and the declaiming (recitation from memory) of great speeches to keep the student's composition activities varied and continually interesting.

PLEASURE AND CHALLENGE IN COMPOSITION

Many students respond to the suggestion of writing for sheer delight. This motive serves in the teaching of limericks, jingles, commercials, fables, slogans, metrical romances, and others. Even though literary artists whose works are being studied by students have approached a subject with great seriousness, students might enjoy writing in the same form but in a humorous way. There is no known literary form in the English discipline which precludes imaginative use. Students might well be motivated to write creatively by suggesting unorthodox subject matters for traditional forms. The titles *Ode to a Cocker Spaniel, Dissertation on Defeat,* and *A Sonnet to Lizzie Bones* suggest some interesting combinations of content and form. Of course, these suggestions are most useful to high school students, since younger children appreciate the ironies and surprises of action rather than the subtle paradoxes of words.

Both the pleasure and challenge of writing and speaking humorously are *real* to students. Little has been done in devising teaching strategies to include the *lighter touch,* where students are led to make their own verbal interpretations of reality.

INNER MOTIVATION AND RHETORIC

Action research has repeatedly shown that students at every educational level respond best to those writing activities which are most intricately related to themselves. The more complex the ties, the better the writing. Classical rhetoric, the ancients' assessment of effective verbal interpretation, is a rich source of ideas related to motivation. The old art, as defined through the writing and practice of Aristotle, Cicero, and Quintilian, taught that there was no greater human skill than to speak and write one's thoughts adequately. To speak well was the epitome of rationality. For this reason, the teaching of rhetoric was synonymous with a liberal education. As a matter of fact, medieval universities offered the trivium of grammar, rhetoric, and logic as the entire four-year undergraduate curriculum.

Rhetoric's value is its humanistic emphasis. It opposes the view that English can be justified on utilitarian grounds. It opposes the theory that a child's cultural background or vocational goal determine his choice of such courses as English for the Disadvantaged, English for Terminal

Students, English for Mechanics Majors, and others. It rejects the thesis that the major purpose of English programs is to teach students to write error-free, acceptable English. The intent of *New Design in the Teaching of English,* however, is to promote a K-Ph.D. English instruction program that is far more than teaching the conventions of standard written English. The main purpose of language arts instruction is defined as *giving students the information, skills, and experience they need to make valid verbal interpretations of reality.*

When students are asked to react to the *know-that* information in the English discipline in a personally meaningful way, they are by this exercise engaged in being and becoming themselves. The student, like all living organisms, grows and develops by dynamic interaction with his environment. His serious personal involvement in synthesizing facts about form and content in the English discipline with his developing self is the process English teachers must encourage in the English classroom.

Whether students are beginners or experts in composition, rhetoric is valuable because it is the art that governs the expression of *selfness.* The representation of one's self, the way a person thinks and feels, is not an easy task. Rhetorical forms and examples of discourse, as well as functional principles for structuring effective expression, are all available in the classical tradition. These suggestions and examples represent man's long struggle to establish a reasonably accurate correspondence between what he is and what he says.

Because all persons enrolled in English programs, whether in kindergarten or college, need further development in fulfilling their potential as verbally creative persons, these persons need a humanistic emphasis in English instruction. It is as necessary for the future mechanic to function in a verbally efficient way as it is for the future doctor. *New Design* holds any English program suspect which does not include the humanistic aspect of verbal art which was so clearly perpetuated through the rhetorical tradition and which is implicit in communication research today.

CREATIVITY AND THE LANGUAGE ARTS

In the tradition of the Western world, education has always meant a leading out or development of a person's power to be and become himself. A child grows and develops not only by interacting with his environment but also by consciously interpreting his experiences. Language is the chief medium through which persons express their ever-changing relationships with external reality. Unless a person can understand and use language to make meaning out of reality, he is seriously handicapped in adjusting to the demands of the world in which he lives. By manipulating language the child exercises the unique creative power of every educable person to make meaning out of reality.[5] By exercising this power more fully and more astutely a person comes gradually to greater mastery over his environment. By making phenomena mean something to himself, the individual, by reason of his creative power, achieves a personally satisfying relationship with reality. "When the self is integrated with the outside world, the mind is profoundly proficient, content, and healthy."[6]

Because well-adjusted persons are inner-oriented, autonomous, and capable of functioning in a positive, self-satisfying way in society, one task of education in its simplest terms is to supply the means by which a child develops the verbal competency essential to his self-fulfillment. A child needs both theoretical information about language and language products and personal experience in using language. Every English program should provide not only for the learning of facts about language but also for the practice of speaking and writing. It is not until *know-that* information is turned into *know-how* skills that the creative power of the student has been challenged.

The language arts are peculiarly adapted to the development of creativity in children. From beginning to end, the components of any language arts program, whether a foreign language or English, are each someone's personal interpretation of reality. *Verbal interpretation is indeed the characteristic mode of language art.* When children learn to decode the graphic or aural representations of these interpretations, they do so precisely to learn how other creative persons have made meaning out of reality and expressed it verbally.

Because the interpretation of reality through verbal skill has a long history, these interpretations fall into identifiable genres and specific verbal art forms. Besides learning what a person has said or written about life, a child also learns *how* it has been said. A truth little discussed in the teaching of English today is that the student needs a command of both the *what* and the *how* of language art if he is to fulfill his creative potential for producing his own interpretations of reality.

Verbal interpretation is often multilevel. For example, a student might interpret the literary criticism of Samuel Johnson, who interpreted Shakespeare, who interpreted an attitude of commoners in Elizabethan times. In every instance however, the interpretation was stamped with the individuating mark of personal creative effort. Though group production is the method of many important achievements today, even some verbal achievements such as textbooks and movie scripts, the method of the literary artist continues to be one of personal creativity.

[5] L. S. Vygotsky, *Thought and Language,* Eugenia Hanfmann and Gertrude Vakar, trans. (New York: Massachusetts Institute of Technology and John Wiley and Sons, Inc., 1962), pp. 1-8.

[6] Michael F. Andrews, ed., *Creativity and Psychological Health* (New York: Syracuse University Press, 1960), p. vi.

RESEARCH IN CREATIVITY

Though recent studies in creativity show considerable divergence regarding a definition of this human quality, the personal nature of the creative act is repeatedly emphasized. Ausubel considers the confusion in establishing a definition of creativity a semantic one.[7] He makes a careful distinction between creativity as a trait inclusive of a wide and continuous range of individual differences and the creative person whose singular talent sets him off qualitatively from others. Although Ausubel's test of true creative production is that the person "must do more than simply produce something that is novel or original in terms of his *own* life history," he accepts the theory of quasi-universal distribution of creative traits:

> It is probably true, however, that general creative abilities, in contrast to creativity *per se,* are more widely distributed and also more susceptible to training. In this sense it can be validly claimed that some creative traits are present in all children; enthusiasts about creativity training, however, tend to imply that potentialities for *creativity* reside in every child, but that their expression is stifled by the culture. It would be more precise and defensible, in my opinion, to state that general creative abilities exist in most children, but that the educational system tends to discourage their development.[8]

The concept of creativity used by E. Paul Torrance embraces a general constellation of intellectual abilities, personality variables, and problem-solving traits. Torrance defines creative thinking as "the process of sensing gaps or disturbing elements; forming ideas or hypotheses concerning them; testing these hypotheses; and communicating the results, possibly modifying and retesting the hypotheses."[9]

The Guilford,[10] Rogers,[11] and Maslow[12] studies identify two basic cognitive or intellective modes: the one simply retentive, predictive, conventional; the other creative, speculative, and unconventional. Whereas Guilford uses the terms *convergent* and *divergent thinking,* Rogers uses *defensiveness* and *openness,* and Maslow uses *safety* and *growth.* All three men, however, distinguish what Thomistic philosophy has traditionally identified as the practical intellect and the speculative intellect, the first

[7] David P. Ausubel, *The Psychology of Meaningful Verbal Learning* (New York and London: Grune and Stratton, 1963), pp. 99-101.

[8] *Ibid.,* p. 103.

[9] E. Paul Torrance, *et al., Assessing the Creative Thinking Abilities of Children* (Minneapolis: Bureau of Educational Research, University of Minnesota, 1960), p. 3.

[10] J. P. Guilford, "Creativity," *American Psychologist,* Vol. 9 (1950), pp. 444-454.

[11] Carl Rogers, *On Becoming a Person* (Boston: Houghton Mifflin Company, 1961).

[12] Abraham Maslow, *Motivation and Personality* (New York: Harper and Brothers, 1954).

mode of operation dealing with *de facto* reality, the second with *de futuro* reality.

Getzels and Jackson, like Guilford, differentiate the highly intelligent from the highly creative adolescent.[13] Using the five creativity measures of word association, uses of things, hidden shapes, fables, and make-up problems to test a whole school population of high IQ adolescents, the researchers state that there is a "relatively low correlation between IQ and performance on tests."[14] Their study of the cognitive style of functioning of these two groups shows that although the creatives are not always the high IQ students, they are consistent in demonstrationg those traits identified through previous research as being associated with the thinking style of creative children. Getzels and Jackson, like Guilford, take a middle position on the role of education in developing creativity, assuming the precontributory effects of heredity and environment:

> For practical purposes we agree with Guilford on a position somewhere between the two extremes (creatives are born: creatives are made). We would adopt as most tenable his belief that education can do a great deal in promoting creative performance, if perhaps not in producing the creative abilities themselves.[15]

Taylor follows Guilford, and also Getzels and Jackson, in identifying the degree of overlap between individuals with high IQ's and those with high creativity scores as approximately 30 percent. Taylor's interpretation of this fact is significant for education:

> If an IQ test is used to select top level talent, about 70 percent of the persons who have the highest 20 percent of the scores on a creativity test battery would be missed.[16]

Both Taylor and Torrance estimate, on the basis of their own and other research, that beyond a cutoff point of 120 IQ, creative thinking abilities rather than higher IQ make the difference in success. Torrance writes:

> Many of the most creative children tested by our staff achieve IQ's in the 120's or slightly under, and most of these children generally achieve quite well. Most such children would not be included in most special programs for gifted children, however.[17]

It is interesting to note that research studies in creativity in the last

[13] Jacob W. Getzels and Philip W. Jackson, *Creativity and Intelligence* (London and New York: John Wiley and Sons, Inc., 1962).
[14] *Ibid.*, p. 20.
[15] *Ibid.*, p. 123.
[16] Calvin W. Taylor, "A Tentative Description of the Creative Individual," *Human Variability and Learning* (Washington, D.C.: Association for Supervision and Curriculum Development, 1961), pp. 68-69.
[17] E. Paul Torrance, *op. cit.*, p. 15.

decade have been generally concerned with only one end of the continuum, the highly talented. Furthermore, only one aspect of creativity,
creative thinking, has been generally investigated. Children have many
talents which escape identification by word tests, guessing games, problem construction, and similar evaluative measures. Some children, for
example, demonstrate manipulative and constructive talent; others give
observable evidence of creative social skills. These talents for making
things and for dealing with the environment, though apparently simple,
are nonetheless true creative endowments. More research should be focused on discovering the creative potential of normal children who test at
the lower end of the IQ scale.

APPLYING RESEARCH IN CREATIVITY

In spite of these various ways of looking at creative power, it must be
noticed that no research challenges the basic notion that creativity is
synonymous with human potential. The late Viktor Lowenfeld, professor
of art education at Pennsylvania State University, presents a statement of
this view:

> I believe that one of the outstanding differences between man
> and animal is that man intentionally creates and the animal does
> not. That implies that every individual is a potential creator. Un-
> fortunately, not everyone's creativeness has been developed so that
> it can properly function. We can, therefore, distinguish between
> the potential creativeness of an individual and his functional crea-
> tiveness.[18]

Michael Andrews repeats this idea:

> Because creativity is a positive, self-integrating force, educa-
> tors committed to the development of youth's potencies are also
> committed to the development of creative power. Creativity is
> then a process of individual experience, of self-actualization, an
> expression of being.[19]

The language arts, repositories of high-order creative verbal productions, are admirably suited to develop the creative power of individuals
at any level. The contents of the verbal arts reveal the whole process of
individual, perceptive experience; the forms of the arts challenge the
production of personal interpretations of reality by means of verbal composition. Students must be taught both the factual, empirical data about
content and form and the skills requisite for personal performance.
(Refer to Figure 3 for a classification of language arts components into
those elements which serve the proximate end of *knowing about* lan-

---

[18] Viktor Lowenfeld, "Basic Aspects of Creative Teaching," *Creativity and Psychological Health* (New York: Syracuse University Press, 1961), p. 130.
[19] Michael F. Andrews, *loc. cit.*

guage, those which serve the final end of *learning how* to achieve creative verbal products, and those which are themselves creative experiences.)

The conceptual structure of *New Design in the Teaching of English* shows that certain components of the language arts program (the science components) best serve as an empirical base for the cognitive and affective behaviors related to knowing—perceiving, defining, interpreting, explaining, justifying, comparing, predicting, and valuing.[20] The structure also shows that other components (the art components) complement *know-that* information by becoming demonstrations of the cognitive and affective processes related to knowledge.

Thus literature, public communication, and linguistics are *fact categories:* the child takes in the information. Functional literature, functional rhetoric, and functional linguistics are skill categories: the child learns how to use facts taken in and does indeed produce verbal artifacts showing the many ways he has made new factual information his own. The experience components in the conceptual structure of *New Design* (see Figure 3) are given space as realities separate from the functional components because they require additional time blocks in the implementation of a curriculum. It must be understood that the *know-that* and *know-how* components are not discrete: functional coding/decoding, functional rhetoric, and functional speech and writing conventions are the functioning or operational aspects of literature, communication, and linguistics. The components are phases of the process of verbal interpretation of reality as every verbal artist knows it. The process goes from empirical fact to artistic production. The intermediary phase is that of instruction in technique. In structuring a curriculum, however, the aspects of a fact category need to be shown as separate entities if the teacher is to understand that different teaching styles are required by different kinds of components. In the ideal English curriculum, a replica of the process of verbal art, what begins as fact ends as performance.

CREATIVITY AND INSTRUCTIONAL METHODS

A distinction between two major classifications of the language art components can, unfortunately, be erased by using a hastily organized teaching method. In one sense, there is homogeneity in all aspects of English because everything is verbal interpretation of reality. However, a true distinction, one implicit in a carefully devised instructional method, is the difference between *facts about* and *facts for.*

In the study of literature, communication, and linguistics, the stu-

[20] Arno Bellack, Herbert Kliebard, *et al., The Language of the Classroom* (New York: Teachers College Press, 1966), pp. 15-40. See also Jerome Bruner, *On Knowing: Essays for the Left Hand.*

dent learns *facts about* reality. The purpose is to know them, that is, to internalize them, to be familiar with information which other English educated persons have found worthy of knowing. In the study of composition the student learns facts for the production of personal verbal responses to reality. The purpose of this kind of information is to use it in creative personal production.

Though there is little research on methodology in the teaching of English, the experienced teacher recognizes the fact that the whole English curriculum can be taught as a *facts about* course. Language and verbal art itself can be taught as the subject of scientific inquiry. The challenge of teaching English at any educational level, however, is that of teaching both the scientific and useful art components of English. The student needs to know the composite of facts in the English discipline not only to be passively well informed, but also to have at his command the knowledge he needs to make valid interpretations of reality.[21]

THE RELATIONSHIP OF SCIENCE AND ART IN THE ENGLISH DISCIPLINE

As the creative craftsman knows, knowledge of materials and forms is as important to success as possession of skills and tools. Unless a creator knows the possibilities and limitations of his forms and media, he can never use them perspicaciously. One reason for studying the scientific aspects of the language arts curriculum is to give the student a sure knowledge (relative to his capacity, of course) to guide his prudential judgments in producing something. Through an analysis of literature, students will learn the unique strengths and limitations of the various forms; an author's techniques will demonstrate what methods are successful in artistic production; language analysis will reveal the resources of the English language as well as its structural peculiarities and regional differences. Because literature contains the forms of verbal interpretation, and language, the media, the student needs to study these elements in a factual and systematic way if he hopes to achieve distinction in his verbal creativity.

Perhaps it is important here to state that the scientific analysis of literature and language is not intrinsically necessary for creative verbal production. It is not important when the user is working in his native language. Children can compose in English; that is, they can produce verbal interpretations of reality without studying literature, public communication, and linguistics. However, a lack of information and experi-

---

[21] David Krathwohl, Benjamin Bloom, and Bertram Masia, *Taxonomy of Educational Objectives, Handbook II: Affective Domain* (New York: David McKay Company, Inc., 1964), pp. 27-38.

ence with scientific, *know-that* information can seriously limit the proficiency and range of a student's creative talent. After all, students need to write about realities that have significance, if they are to write well. The real experience of many students, however, is often limited both in quality and depth. Vicarious experience gained through the reading of literature appropriate to the real response potential of students strengthens the creative power of young writers and helps to validate their comments on reality.[22]

This is not to contradict the view that children can compose without studying the endless facts related to the form, content, and method of literary creation, literary criticism, communication, and linguistics. The important point is that the *know-that* aspects of the English discipline are as response-oriented as the *know-how* components. The student, however, does not need the factual matter of the discipline *before* he can begin composing. He has his own direct, physical, social, and psychological confrontation with reality to write and talk about.

SEQUENTIAL INSTRUCTION

In terms of adjusting a multicomponent English curriculum to children's abilities, *know-how* information should usually precede *know-that* kind. Children do not need a detailed understanding of whole units of factual information on a particular subject before they can be asked to produce a verbal artifact. What particular groups of children need at a particular time can only be determined by the classroom teacher who knows his students well. The young child develops verbal facility by exercise in verbal expression through the verbal art forms he can understand.

Facility in verbal expression presupposes experience in reading and listening to language products. The greater the experience, the greater the facility. Although there is no research at the high school level to show the extent to which interrelations exist or can be effected among the language arts, the Loban study which analyzes language used by 338 selected children from K-6 shows positive interrelationships between reading and written language and between oral and written language. Loban explains:

> As the subjects continue into the upper years of elementary school, a high interrelation between writing and reading becomes apparent. The superior group in writing has by far the highest reading achievement and the highest teachers' rating. Even more striking is the fact that *every* subject ranked superior in writing is

[22] Dwight L. Burton, "Literature and the Heightened Mind," in *Teaching English in Today's High Schools* (New York: Holt, Rinehart and Winston, Inc., 1966), p. 30.

reading above his chronological age; every subject ranked illiterate or primitive in writing is *reading below* his chronological age . . . As can be seen on every statistical measure, one fact is extremely clear in the present study: those who read well also write well; those who read poorly also write poorly.

In addition to the relation between reading and writing, data accumulated in this study show a high relation between reading and oral language. The scattergram shown for grade six indicates a definite positive relation between these two elements of language with the pattern again being that a subject who excells in reading also excells in oral language. However, it does not so clearly follow that the poor reader will also be poor in oral language.[23]

It would be a mistake to conclude from this study that the panacea for language arts deficiency in the high school is simply to teach more reading in elementary grades. Ruth Strickland has repeatedly emphasized the need for an integrated English program, one in which the skills buttress and supplement one another:

Writing is one of the language arts, and it is highly dependent for its growth on the growth in the other language arts. The quality of writing is closely related to the quality of speech.[24]

Though retarded readers need remedial instruction, the fact must be remembered that adolescents also have genuine needs for broad information about reality as well as insistent needs to make some personal synthesis out of the ever increasing complexities of their world. The fact that students may be reading above or below grade level is not a sufficient reason for limiting the variety of *know-that* and *know-how* information at the high school level. Increased or decreased amounts of these subject matters can be justified by the ability and learning styles of various groups, but the omission of one component of the language arts curriculum means a deficiently trained English student, a student for whom the int rrelationships of the language arts have not been allowed to function freely.

CREATIVITY AND THE DISADVANTAGED

To force a student, especially a disadvantaged one, into an English program that consists exclusively of remedial reading exercises seems somewhat unenlightened in terms of present knowledge about the English curriculum and the nature of learning. A single-component program denies the child the right to work creatively. In spite of his handi-

[23] Walter D. Loban, *The Language of Elementary School Children* (Champaign, Illinois: National Council of Teachers of English, 1963), pp. 69-74.
[24] Ruth G. Strickland, "Evaluating Children's Composition," *Children's Writing: Research in Composition and Related Skills* (Champaign, Illinois: National Council of Teachers of English, 1960), p. 65.

caps, the student in the ordinary classroom can do something wonderful with language: he can talk. This in itself is enough verbal skill to begin making personal creative interpretations of the world. The major aim of the English program, the student's satisfactory rapprochement with reality, can thus be achieved in spite of his failure to interpret graphicemic symbols proficiently.

Louis Fliegler, coordinator of education for exceptional children at the University of Denver, repeats the idea that creativity is a universally human attribute inherent in man himself rather than some quality of man such as intelligence or skill in reading.

> As previously suggested, a review of past events shows that the movement of life is forward. The fundamental aim of existence is to improve the evolution of man. Creativity can then be interpreted as a natural urge to develop and unfold. . . .
> All individuals are creative in diverse ways and to different degrees. Essentially, creativity is not some mystical process which occurs only with the few, but exists within each individual. Creativity is within the realm of each individual depending upon the area of expression and capability of the individual.[25]

There is little reason to believe that the culturally disadvantaged child is not capable of creativity. The poorly languaged child is a reflection of his limited experiences with verbal interpretation, nothing more. Given the right kind of instruction and compensatory language experiences, the nonstandard speaker develops verbal competency and high order creative verbal behavior like other children.

CREATIVITY AND CREATIVE WRITING

All writing is a high type creative act involving organization, synthesis, and verbal coding. A good language arts program is uniquely suited to the exercise and development of individual creativity because its purposes, its content, and its method are related to creative enterprise. Because the student's effort in composition work, both oral and written, can be nothing except creative, the term *creative writing* might well be dropped from the lexicon of useful terms in the teaching of English. This peculiar designate was valid before 1952, when the research efforts of Guilford, Torrance, Maslow, Mead, Ausubel, Anderson, Alberty, Lowenfeld, Fliegler, Allport, Rogers, Getzels, Jackson, Taylor, Mooney, and others had not yet clarified the concept of creativity and its implications for education. Today it serves only to suggest a teacher's limited experience in his discipline.

[25] Louis A. Fliegler, "Dimensions of the Creative Process," *Creativity and Psychological Health* (New York: Syracuse University Press, 1961), p. 14.

CREATIVITY AND THE STUDENT

English students at every educational level should be taught why all verbal art is a product of creative competency. They must understand that oral interpretations of reality as well as written interpretations depend for their intrinsic excellence on the pre-expressional process of *organizing data*. The way a person internally orders his experience, integrating it with his overall knowing-feeling structure, creates the distinctiveness every worthwhile utterance has. Valuing one's own power to create verbally motivates improved production.

As soon as students are old enough to be interested in the process of verbal artistry, it might be well for English teachers to explain how *know-how* data serves to turn plain *know-that* fact into artistic statement. Already in the intermediate grades, children are motivated to high level English work by understanding that their own language arts education is patterned after that of literary artists.

NAMING AND USING TRADITIONAL LITERARY FORMS

Since all writing is creative, verbal art forms, whether oral or written, should be designated by the *name of the form*. Whether referred to in the *know-that* category of the English components or in the *know-how* division, literary forms must be called by name by both teachers and students. No person can consider himself educated in his discipline or trade unless he has learned to understand and use the terminology (jargon, perhaps) common to that particular activity. *The English student must gradually achieve mastery of all literary terms related formally to the creation, criticism, and communication of verbal art.* Some language products which any English educated person should be able to know and imitate include a variety of forms such as ballads, book reviews, story critiques, oral reports, newspaper editorials, dialogues, commercials, declamations, essays, campaign speeches, skits, radio plays, lyric poems, metrical tales, jingles, after-dinner speeches, research reports, term papers, debate speeches, panel reports, symposium papers, rhetorical analyses, poetry analyses, short stories, news stories, news broadcasts, book blurbs, announcer scripts, summaries, fables, magazine articles, letters, diaries, autobiographies, biographical sketches, travelogues, limericks, advertisements, monologues, grammatical analyses, and others.

Performance in oral and written composition, then, should be the goal in teaching the *know-how* components of the English curriculum. Many identifiable forms of verbal creation should be used to challenge the student's power to produce his own language products, and many kinds of evaluative measures should be employed to assess these individual art forms. Whether a student is composing a description to be dictated to the first grade teacher or whether the Ph.D. candidate is preparing material for his doctoral orals, his work must be evaluated in terms of personal verbal creation. This is the end of instruction in English language art, that all students develop appropriate verbal creativity through a study of the discipline called English.

III

Literature and Literary Criticism in K-College English

As theory is related to practice, so is literary criticism related to literature. When the literary critic exercises his function of analyzing and interpreting a literary work, he does so by referring to specific attributes of that work—its structure, its language, its allusions, its historicity, its conventions, its genre. Were it not for a body of literary criticism as old as literature itself, which has gradually formulated a universal concept of what particular works *ought to be,* the forms of literature known today would be indistinguishable. It is because the combined efforts of literary critics of the Western world have identified the general characteristics of separate literary forms that aspiring artists can learn these characteritics and create with confidence. Even writing experimentally and trying to create new forms necessitates a knowledge of the traditional forms.

Literary theory has relevance not only to literary form but to technique as well. How a writer creates, his method of interpreting experience through verbal symbol, is important to the critic whose function it is to understand and explain the artist's method. As in form, so in method, the work of many critics of the past and present has resulted in universal knowledge of appropriate methods. For this reason new artists can know these traditional methods and can either use them with assurance or consciously depart from them.

Because human ingenuity is inexhaustible, writers will always continue to create new forms and to devise new methods. Critics, then, will also continue to function as interpreters, seeking by means of their own creative power to make meaning out of these new realities. In so doing they continue to extend the body of literary criticism while adjusting and redelineating the traditional concepts of form and method. Because the work of the literary critic demands insight into verbal art, knowledge of form and method, and verbal creativity, literary criticism is itself a kind of literature.

53

LITERARY STUDIES IN HIGH SCHOOL

In the high school classroom, literature and literary criticism can be taught as complements of one another. The students can then see their literary heritage as a totality. Since many works by critics, such as Sidney's *Defense of Poesy*, Johnson's *Life of Shakespeare*, T. S. Eliot's *Tradition and the Individual Talent*, have the necessary qualities of literary distinction, it seems not unreasonable to include the *literature* of literary criticism in the high school program.

The high school student's own creative potential as a verbal artist also suggests the teaching of criticism. Unless the student learns the traditional forms and methods used by writers, he cannot produce acceptable work. Even the imaginative genius cannot begin to create unless he knows what he is making and how to make it. Although there may be value in permitting free, formless, verbal expression through impressionistic narratives or "poems," a well-integrated English curriculum includes more than such writing. The Language Committee of the School and College Conference on English states:

> If the compostion finally produced does not exhibit form, design, order, intellectual coherence as well as expressiveness, the Conference does not see what progress is being made toward any rational educational goal. The Conference believes that all the writing a student does well involves both thought and imagination, intellectual order and expressiveness.[1]

It is precisely the form of a literary work that gives it an identifiable structure. If someone is to write a sonnet, he must conform to the *pattern of language and thought* that the sonnet represents. But the form is not only a stricture; it is also an effective agent of communication because it carries an accumulation of associated images. The young writer needs both the help gained through using a form familiar to his audience and the discipline imposed by a form which the best minds have used successfully. The Language Committee of the School and College Conference on English makes this point:

> The writing of a poem or story of any degree of accomplishment . . . demands the sense of order and structure, design and coherence; it calls for the exercise of a certain kind of logic. . . . It will be more valuable if the writer learns to subject imagination to discipline and orderly progress. The familiar essay must find form to steer its informality; the story and the poem must possess design and direction, even for the most modest flight.[2]

---

[1] George Winchester Stone, Jr., ed., *Issues, Problems, and Approaches in the Teaching of English* (New York: Holt, Rinehart and Winston, 1961), pp. 36-37.
[2] *Ibid.*

Besides offering the high school student a complete notion of literature and helping to develop his creative potential, literary criticism can also aid the student in understanding what he reads. The tools and analytic techniques which the critic uses to understand literature can also be used by the high school student. As a matter of fact, few high school texts exclude the use of critical terms and techniques. However, because they are presented as bits of information apart from the whole subject of criticism they tend to be unimportant to the student. If the criticism of literature is to be a meaningful study it must be taught as a *know-that* component of the English curriculum and practiced as a *know-how* element. Critical terms can help a student understand literature only when they are used in relation to the discipline of literary criticism and applied to various literary works. It is through the analytic method of literary criticism that both teacher and student discover the forms, the techniques, the subject matter, and the meaning that a literary artist has embodied in his work. For this reason it seems reasonable to propose that teaching about literature should include teaching about literary criticism.

In many high school classrooms English teachers assume the entire responsibility for analyzing and understanding literary works. Students are asked to follow the analysis and to see the meaning which the teacher has ferreted out. If the student himself were given the tools of criticism, terminology, and technique, he could, in many instances, perform the task independently. Learning the terms and understanding their use is a *know-that* aspect of English education; using the terms in discovering form and method for oneself is a *know-how* aspect of English education. When the student can make his own valid criticisms of verbal interpretation, using the forms and methods he has learned, the teacher has *taught criticism* thoroughly.

It is by *practicing criticism* that the student gains power in understanding what he reads. There can be no apathy here on the student's part, no quiet acceptance of what he may or may not understand, if he is required to *produce* a critical essay of some kind. By encouraging a student to exercise his knowledge the teacher affords him the opportunity of clarifying his *know-that* information and strengthening his creative verbal power. This aim is one which Alfred North Whitehead has often discussed:

> In training a child to activity of thought, above all things we must beware of what I will call "inert ideas"—that is to say, ideas that are merely received into the mind without being utilized, or tested, or thrown into fresh combinations.[3]

[3] Alfred North Whitehead, *The Aims of Education* (New York: The Macmillan Company, 1929), p. 13.

By practicing the techniques and using the terms of the literary critic, the student understands both literature and literary criticism more thoroughly.

CRITICISM AND CROSS-COMPONENT INTEGRATION

Knowing and using the skills of literary criticism can effect a desirable integration not only between literature and criticism, but also between literature and rhetoric. Because rhetoric has traditionally been concerned with the practical art of discursive prose, it is not, strictly speaking, related to such verbal art forms as the novel and the essay. These forms developed after medieval times and they were not governed by the classical canons of either rhetoric or poetry. Literary criticism, however, is discursive prose at its best. In seeking to convince his audience that his interpretation has merit, the critic has recourse to every rhetorical scheme available. It is sometimes difficult to deny the similarity between the *literary case* argued by the critic and the *legal case* presented by an attorney. In the last analysis, narration, argumentation, description, and exposition are the basic prose methods used by all persons in making verbal interpretations of reality. As soon as a student knows the basic terms and techniques of criticism, he can apply them by analyzing a literary work and expressing himself through appropriate rhetorical modes.

Such integration in the teaching of language arts gives the student a command of subject matter and a development of skill he might otherwise lack. It follows an educational dictum suggested by Whitehead: "Do not teach too many subjects. What you teach, teach thoroughly."[4] Whitehead explains the need for integrated teaching as follows:

> The result of teaching small parts of a large number of subjects is the passive reception of disconnected ideas, not illumined with any spark of vitality. Let the main ideas which are introduced into a child's education be few and important, and let them be thrown into every combination possible. The child should make them his own, and should understand their application here and now in the circumstances of his actual life.[5]

Probably no skill serves a student's academic and practical needs better than an aptitude for correct verbal interpretation. To know which techniques to use and to know how to use them effectively are important skills not only in school where most learning is verbal, but also in practical life where the products of the mass media of communication demand ever-new analysis and evaluation. Life itself with its incessant demand for social interaction requires the formulation and expression of myriad

[4] *Ibid.,* p. 14.
[5] *Ibid.*

evaluative judgments. When a student realizes the practicality of learning how to analyze and understand literature and how to express his opinions and judgments with rhetorical skill, the problem of motivation is for the most part solved. Children tend to accept what relates to themselves. Interest, in fact, varies with the degree of association or identification a child can project into his activities. Integrating the teaching of literary criticism and literature with rhetoric is a step forward toward the solution of the problem of motivation which Whitehead says stems from "the fatal disconnection of subjects which kills the vitality of our modern curriculum.[6]

INTEGRATION IN THE ELEMENTARY SCHOOL

If genuine integration is to be effected in teaching the English discipline, the interrelationships among the various components must be learned and practiced by the child at an early age. Small children can begin to understand and use the key factors basic to literary criticism already in the primary grades. For example, the notion of theme (the universal truth embodied in a story) can be explored by questions similar to the following:

> What is the author trying to tell me in this story?
> What important idea is the author sharing with me?
> What will I always remember about this story?
> How did the author try to make me remember his main idea?
> Does this author have the same idea about life that I do?

Similarly, the concept of conflict (the struggle for mastery between opposing forces) can be developed by questions like the following:

> Is there a conflict in this story?
> Who seems to be struggling in this book?
> What is the main character trying to do?
> Who is struggling against the main character?
> Was the conflict in this story true to life? Why?
> Am I pleased that the conflict turned out as it did?

By structuring the questions so that the child asks them of himself, and by using the children's own literature, the teacher can give the young students enough *know-that* and *know-how* information to stimulate genuine personal interpretation.[7]

[6] *Ibid.*, p. 18.
[7] Questions and book titles useful in teaching literary criticism in the elementary school are available from Mrs. Louise Thompson, Language Arts Supervisor, Frederick County Public Schools, Frederick, Maryland.

By learning and using critical concepts at an early age, the child develops insight into the meaning of verbal art. His gradually increasing knowledge of authors' technique will result in heightened appreciation and involvement in reading, composing, discussing, and valuing verbal art. If discrimination and good taste in language art are to mark the English educated man, then the critical faculty should be exercised already at the primary levels of education.

THE PROBLEM OF ARTIFICIAL CORRELATION

When literary criticism, literature, and rhetoric effect an identifiable unity in the English discipline, a singular benefit results: a misguided correlation is obviated.[8] In the past, one of the greatest problems in teaching English was the accumulation of miscellaneous subject matter pretending to be English. Although literature is a humanistic study, sharing the common aim of all humane letters, it has, nonetheless, its own intrinsic values and purposes. The Literature Committee of the School and College Conference on English clarifies this point:

> The student who is spontaneously interested in his civics course may be led to a greater respect for literature through the study of its relations with society. Yet we must remember that literature does not exist simply as an opportunity for correlation. Just as the study of civics has its own important values in its own right, to which literary studies might rightly contribute, so literature has its own characteristic value which the student should be led to feel for its own sake. Certainly literature is in part a record of social conditions, conflicts, and ideals. The student should be made to see as much as he can of the relations between literary works and the ages and nations which produced them. But to use literature only as an adjunct to civics or to any other study would be to put aside entirely the special realm of value contained in literature itself as an art.[9]

When literary criticism, literature, and rhetoric are taught in an integrated way, there is neither need nor time for artificial correlations with other subject matter areas. Every component of the language arts program, whether it is a component of literature, communication, linguistics, or composition, is a necessary part of the whole discipline called English. To omit the teaching of one component is to weaken the total effect of the discipline. To repeat and to use the components in interrelated ways is to strengthen the total effect of the discipline.

[8] George Winchester Stone, Jr., *op. cit.*, p. 44.
[9] *Ibid.*

TEACHING LITERARY APPRECIATION

When English is taught in an integrated way, without needless digression into other subject areas, the most difficult aspect of English teaching, literary appreciation, becomes feasible. Good taste, a discerning sensitivity in literary matters, can neither be cultivated nor expressed in a worthy manner unless the student has had a rich personal experience with literature. The twenty-two years comprising a complete English education are too short a time to develop the skill of discernment unless every opportunity for an integrated study of literature is used. The student must experience literature as reading matter, as verbal art, as the embodiment of man's highest aspirations, as a tradition of culture, as a mode of communication, as a compendium of linguistic data, as an intricate graphic code, as an exemplification of grammatical and rhetorical principles, as an opportunity for personal judgment and self-expression, and as a pure delight. An integrated English program consisting of both *know-that* and *know-how* elements provides a wealth of experiences when the natural correlations among composition, linguistics, communication, and literature are utilized.

An excess of literature, allowed in the English program because its subject matter interests the student, can defeat the development of literary appreciation. If a student continues to read only for entertainment or to acquire information without receiving instruction in criticism and appreciation, he will remain on a reading plateau, never confronting *literature as an art,* with its characteristic mode of interpretation, its specialized forms, and its inherent discipline. This confrontation can be brought about through an integrated English program where free reading and classroom instruction proceed simultaneously, where the student not only reads independently but also reads under guidance, answering specific questions, noting specific techniques, and expressing his discoveries and reactions through his own verbal products. There has been a tendency in grades 5 to 12 to encourage extensive reading with little attention given to literary criticism and composition. Especially with the noncollege-bound student, teachers seem to have neglected the investigation of the forms and methods which a literary artist uses to accomplish his purpose, stressing instead a free reading of selections suited to the student's present tastes.

Students at any educational level should be encouraged to exercise *their right to read;* however, if they are to understand and appreciate literature, they need opportunities to apply the terms and techniques of literary criticism through written composition. Not only must the student be taught how to look deeply into a piece of literature, he must also be led to express his reactions in writing, inferior though his efforts may be.

Edwin Sauer emphasizes the need for composition work for high school students particularly:

> I have invited the reader to question the traditional objectives of the writing program, principally the assumption that writing is only for the superior student, an effort to give him stylistic elegance and charm. The objectives of the high school writing program go far beyond this, and their primary interest is the clarification and organization of thought. The writing man is, first of all, the thinking man.[10]

It is the necessity of writing that often motivates thinking. With most students, the need to express a thought in writing encourages the discovery of something to say. When a student is shown how other men, literary critics, have used certain techniques and terms to discover and report important information about literature, he too is encouraged to make discoveries and to express them in writing. By shuttling from literature, to literary criticism, to composition, the student gradually comes to formulate his personal concept of what literature is and what aspects of it deserve admiration. When linguistics and public communication can be brought in, a high-level integration has been achieved. This is literary appreciation in practical terms; it is the student's ability to discern and to value the important elements that create the meaning of a work of literary art.

INTEGRATION, FREE READING, AND TOTAL LANGUAGE SKILLS

An integrated English program does not exclude a vigorous free reading program. In some instances the combined pressures of school work and extracurricular activities may curtail the number of books a student may freely choose to read outside of class. However, the English teacher's selection and reaction to books help to influence the student's taste. "Essentially, he is a guide who leads pupils into a land he knows well and loves greatly."[11] To abdicate leadership in this area is to lose the potential influence which a lifetime of personal experience with books might exert on a student. The teaching of literary criticism can support and enrich the free reading program by furnishing the student with *things to say* about his book. When he interprets literature he will have not only the vocabulary he needs to communicate his ideas, but he will also have something to discuss besides the plot of the story. The combined motivation of personal criticism, of organizing something to

---

[10] Edwin H. Sauer, *English in the Secondary School* (New York: Holt, Rinehart and Winston, 1961), p. vi.

[11] Wilfred Eberhart, *et al., Manual for Reading-Literature,* Book 3 (Evanston, Illinois: Row, Peterson and Company, 1955), p. 53.

say, and of using new techniques to discover information can effect student involvement of great educational value.

A number of educational leaders have cautioned teachers to exercise restraint in their preference for teaching *only* literature, rather than all the language arts components. In a national survey conducted from 1958 to 1961, the National Council of Teachers of English found that ten practices were common to schools producing superior English students. J. N. Hook, director of the survey, summarizes these results, two of which are directly related to an integrated English program:

> Require considerable amounts of writing from students, with much of the writing on nonpersonal subjects.
>
> Offer English courses that balance instruction in literature and composition about evenly.[12]

Edwin Sauer also believes in a well-integrated English program, and warns against an excess of literature:

> The first assertion that might be made about the teaching of literature in the high school is that there is probably too much of it. As Dr. James B. Conant says, skill in composition is surely our first need in today's world; training in the clear, orderly expression of thought should be, in my judgment, the first subject of the curriculum.[13]

Helen C. White writes:

> Specialization is, of course, the way of all modern technical and scientific civilization, and with the advancement of knowledge, an inevitable consequence of our very achievements; yet I am not at all sure that its effects are altogether happy in our field.[14]

The teaching of literature which does not include training in literary criticism and composition can result in wide reading that lacks direction and coherence. Whether this reading is left to the student's free choice or whether it is guided by a teacher who loves literature and hopes to share his enthusiasm, it must serve some educational purpose besides entertainment or uncritical appreciation. Hans P. Guth writes:

> Certainly, the teacher must make his students feel he cares about literature; he must communicate to them his sense of its significance and excitement. But he cannot do so by teaching that it is an extended variation on the theme of "I like what I like." He needs a workmanlike grasp of what makes literature what it is.[15]

[12] *The National Interest and the Teaching of English* (Champaign, Illinois: National Council of Teachers of English, 1961), p. 114.

[13] Edwin H. Sauer, *op. cit.*, p. 141.

[14] Helen C. White, *Changing Styles in Literary Studies* (Cambridge: Cambridge University Press, 1963), p. 23.

[15] Hans P. Guth, *English Today and Tomorrow* (Englewood Cliffs, New Jersey: Prentice-Hall, Inc., 1964), p. 219.

W. K. Wimsatt, Jr. agrees that it is not enough to talk about literary significance and value in vague, inspirational terms. The staple commitments of the teacher include the following:

> *Explanation* . . . of the explicit and clearly ascertainable but perhaps obscure or disguised meaning of words; *description* . . . of the poem's structure and parts, its shape and colors, and its historical relations; *explication* . . . the turning of such description as far as possible into meaning.[16]

These factual statements about literature presuppose the method of critical analysis. They also suggest that the writing which students do in connection with their literary studies follows basic rhetorical methods.

A literature, then, that is taught with critical intent and discussed through oral and written composition seems well suited to develop a student's literary skill and appreciation. When a free reading program is conducted parallel to formal critical instruction, the student can be given an increasingly deeper, more personal, and more dynamic experience with literature. Whether the free reading activity takes the shape of generally known individualized programs in the elementary school[17] or of creative preseminar readings in graduate school, *New Design* recommends that the input of reading be given a new personal format by the critical verbal productions (output) of the student. The need for restructuring information in terms of one's total cognitive-affective make-up and the need for expressing these creations verbally is construed by *New Design* to be necessary for genuine learning in the discipline of English. Literary criticism offers method, mode, and motivation for personal interpretation of literature.

LITERARY CRITICISM IN THE K-PH.D. ENGLISH SEQUENCE

There is a wealth of material clarifying the terms, concepts, and methods of literary criticism. Recently, considerable information has appeared in periodicals and booklet publications of the National Council of Teachers of English on the literary criticism of literature for adolescents. Each English teacher will use some unique synthesis of information he has acquired through academic courses and personal experience with

---

[16] W. K. Wimsatt, Jr., "What to Say About a Poem," *College English*, Vol. XXIV (February, 1963), p. 381.

[17] Several standard references might be useful to elementary and junior high school English teachers: Walter B. Barbe, *Educator's Guide to Personalized Reading Instruction* (New Jersey: Prentice-Hall, Inc., 1961); Alice Mill, ed., *Individualizing Reading Practices* (New York: Teachers College, Columbia University, 1958); Ruth Strickland, *The Language Arts in the Elementary School* (Boston: D. C. Heath and Company, 1957).

literature. There may be one caution needed here: teachers should avoid both dogmatism and discipleship. The vocabulary pertaining to any art is in continuous reassessment by the practitioners of the art. Terms, then, will change just as philosophies and theories of the art will change. Although high school students are generally interested in *schools of criticism,* willing to learn the major differences between *new critics* and *traditionalists,* the facts that students need are not those which cause controversy but those which foster agreement and illumination. Much academic criticism, the product of professional scholarship in the humanities, is far removed from the needs and interests of the high school student.

To guide the selection of material to be used as subject matter in literary criticism several distinctions must be made. First of all, literary criticism is not a kind of scientific skepticism which approaches all reality negatively. The word *criticism* has a negative connotation, unfortunately, but there seems to be no better term available at the present time. *Evaluation* is a poor substitute as a general term because in literary criticism its specific denotation is judicial criticism. Although there are four levels of criticism: reaction, commentary, judicial criticism, and academic criticism,[18] the high school student will work mainly on the first two levels and occasionally on the third. Younger students will be exercised mainly in commentary, whereas college and graduate students will be concerned with all kinds of criticism, including genuine judicial evaluation.

Reaction is the first level of literary criticism. Teaching high school students to express their reactions to literature is not difficult when they have already had considerable practice in the elementary school, nor is judicial and academic criticism too difficult for levels 14-22 when personal reaction and commentary have been creative verbal enterprises since kindergarten. A reaction is a personal, impressionistic response to literature. It concerns individual taste, sensitivity, or feeling. Little objective evidence is cited for the impression, or if some is given it carries little intellectual weight. The little girl who said, "This books tells more about penguins than I need to know," was expressing her reaction.

Commentary, the second of four levels of literary criticism, is probably the most widely used aspect of literary criticism. It can be subjective or objective in focus, but its distinguishing mark is its concern for the literary work itself. Its aim is not to arrive at a judgment regarding the relative merit of a literary piece, but rather to arrive at an understanding of it. Some of the concepts with which both elementary and high school students should be familiar in order to write intelligent

---

[18] Northrop Frye, "Literary Criticism," *The Aims and Methods of Scholarship in Modern Languages and Literatures* (New York: Modern Language Association, 1963), pp. 57-69.

commentary include the following: theme, characterization, plot, dialogue, conflict, imagery, diction, metaphor, rhythm, meter, prose, poetry, genre, convention, tragedy, myth, archetype, tone, persona, and others. Some of the *approaches* to a literary work (these are examinations focused on a particular kind of inquiry) might include the biographical, canonical, cultural, psychological, stylistic, interpretive, or historical.[19]

Although the various approaches which a teacher uses to lead students to understanding and worthwhile comment on literary art are almost self-explanatory, a distinction might be made between the historical approach to literature and literary history. The historical approach concerns a particular work under examination. Using the analytical and relatively objective method of historical research, the student or teacher looks for internal or external facts in the work which if explained by further study would illumine the work as a whole. These facts are not only dates but also ideas which might be traceable to certain eras, institutions, traditions, or facts from the classical and Biblical heritage. When the facts are found, they are clarified by further research and related to general commentary on the work in question.

Literary history is the scholarly discipline which describes and explains the development of mankind as it is expressed in literature. In no sense is it critical in intention, and this marks it off clearly from the simple historical approach which is an aspect of literary criticism. Robert E. Spiller writes:

> The literary historian is a historian among other historians and his function is to write the history of man as revealed in literature, as the functions of other historians are to write the history of man as revealed in government, commerce, ideas, painting, architecture, or any other kinds of human expression in act or form.[20]

Literary history has less appeal for elementary children than for high school and college students. As a distinguishable component of the high school English curriculum, it has special relevance for several reasons. First, the method of the literary historian is part science and part art. His search for fact is an objective, scholarly one, while his presentation and interpretation of fact is a creative one. This dual skill consisting of the accuracy of the scientist and creativity of the artist is the same skill which is envisioned as an aim of the teaching of literature to the high school student. Furthermore, the method of the literary historian is the same method that the literary critic adopts temporarily when he chooses a

---

[19] Francis Lee Utley, *et al., Bear, Man, and God* (New York: Random House, 1964), pp. 117-119.
[20] Robert E. Spiller, "Literary History," *The Aims and Methods of Scholarship in Modern Languages and Literatures* (New York: Modern Association, 1963), p. 41.

historical approach to literature. To understand the method as a tool of literary history is to strengthen its use as a technique of literary criticism. Finally, literary history enriches the study of literature by defining the works of literary art of the past, by presenting the story of their development, by describing the influences that impelled these changes, and by placing a work in its correct chronological sequence as well as in its right context of place and authorship.

Probably the greatest single value in teaching a proportionate amount of literary history in the K-Ph.D. English sequence is the sense of historicity it imparts to students. To look at anything in its historical perspective is to look at it wisely and calmly, for a knowledge of the past proportions a judgment of the present. Especially in the study of literary art, students can neither assess accurately nor appreciate fully a piece of literature unless they can see it as part of a continuous literary tradition. The historical sense which T. S. Eliot says "involves a perception, not only of the pastness of the past, but of its presence" is what students gain through the study of literary history.[21]

Commentary, then, can be enriched by means of both the method and the factual data of literary history. With the vast possibilities for comment implied in the seven approaches to literature (Utley), with the analytic method of the literary historian, and with the terms and concepts of the literary critic, the student has much material to use in developing skill in understanding and appreciating literature. Furthermore, he has inexhaustible resources for developing writing skill in all the basic rhetorical modes: narration, argumentation, description, and exposition. For this reason, there seems to be little purpose in asking students before level fourteen to write judicial criticism.

Judicial criticism, the third level of literary criticism, is the scholarly effort to evaluate a literary work. Since evaluation necessitates good taste and a clear intellectual apprehension of the nature of the thing being judged, students cannot be expected to make valid scholarly judgments about literature. Their taste is as yet unformed, and their knowledge of literature is severely limited; hence, it is unlikely that they are able to make a valid assessment of a particular piece of literary art. The best students can do is to follow the judgments of other judicial critics, but this practice defeats the goals of a creative English program. Secondhand generalizations which are frequently contradictory and often wrong discourage and confuse the high school student. Being forced to rely on the judgment of others and to use stereotype labels which he does not understand, the student soon loses confidence in his own power to understand and appreciate literature. As Hans P. Guth says:

[21] T. S. Eliot, "Tradition and the Individual Talent," *Selected Essays* (New York: Harcourt, Brace and World, Inc., 1932), p. 6.

> Too often such labels—*the artificiality of courtly love, the deca-*
> *dence of the Jacobean playwrights, the immorality of the Restora-*
> *tion stage*—keep the student from coming to grips with the com-
> plex patterns of feeling and form in the actual works.[22]

Before students gain some specialization as English majors (levels 14-
22), they should not be asked to act as judicial critics. They, themselves,
see the futility of trying to evaluate what literary scholarship and popular good taste have established as great works of literary art. They also
realize the limitations of their own knowledge. This, in the final instance,
is what forces them to echo critics' judgments which they do not understand. As Northrop Frye says, "What gives a judge the right to be on a
bench is knowledge of law."[23] Students in high school and freshman
English courses realize that they are too poorly equipped as historians,
sociologists, psychologists, philosophers, novelists, or poets to approach a
work of art and judge its literary merit. However, they can be encouraged
to read serious judicial criticism without reference to practicing it. By
reading this kind of criticism, which ordinarily has an excellent discursive method, they will probably accept the truth of the following conclusion:

> Judicial criticism is based on good taste, and good taste is a skill
> founded by practice on the knowledge the critic has. Lapses of
> taste and value judgment, when made by highly experienced
> critics, are usually the result of insufficient knowledge of litera-
> ture. Consequently knowledge always has the power of veto over
> taste.[24]

Academic criticism, the fourth and highest level of literary criticism
is, like judicial evaluation, beyond the competency of the ordinary high
school student. Concerned with understanding rather than assessment,
academic criticism examines a work of literary art in the largest context
possible, life itself. Transcending the judicial, the historical, the contemporary, and the contextual, academic criticism investigates the larger
questions: why man produces literature, what it does for society, and how
it is related to other uses of the mother tongue. As Northrop Frye says:

> This is the point at which criticism moves into the conception
> described by Matthew Arnold as culture, where the study of the
> best that has been thought and said becomes an organized force in
> society, dissolving its grosser inequalities, refining manners, disci-
> plining the emotions as well as the intellect, and assimilating the
> actualities to the ideals of human civilization.[25]

It seems wise, then, for younger students (K-13 and probably 14-16)
not to practice either judicial or academic criticism. Reaction and com-

[22] Hans P. Guth, *op. cit.,* p. 229.
[23] Northrop Frye, *op. cit.,* p. 60.
[24] *Ibid.,* p. 62.
[25] *Ibid.,* p. 68.

mentary are well within the knowledge and skill of elementary, secondary, and first year college students, and these types of literary criticism offer an interesting and inexhaustible area of practice. There seems to be no reason, however, why the high school and freshman college student should be denied the pleasure and instruction that come from reading judicial and academic criticism. The controversial aspect of much judicial criticism acts as a stimulus to further reading. The genuine creativity and stylistic perfection of some academic criticism proves to the student that criticism and literature are related as theory is to practice. The more discerning students will see that in some instances the knowledge and creative skill of the critic have become the vision and genius of the artist.

LITERATURE AND THE KNOW-HOW SKILLS

Like literary criticism, literature is a separate and important component of the high school English curriculum. Although reading skills emphasized in the elementary school are practiced and further developed through instruction in the high school, reading in the secondary school is not ordinarily taught as a *know-how* subject. David H. Russell has a statement which clarifies this point:

> Although not all linguistic scientists accept the point of view, most school people agree that reading is essentially a process of getting meanings from printed symbols.[26]

At the high school level, teachers assume that students can interpret printed symbols; they are directly concerned with the student's power to interpret ideas. It is the student's *response* to literature (integrated with reading experience) that is the focal point of instruction. It is the student's *understanding* and *appreciation* of literature that motivates most literary study in the high school.

An English educator would be ill-advised to ignore the problem of retarded reading at any educational level. Whether a student reads below grade norms in junior high school or in first year college, an English teacher must adjust an existing curriculum to the needs of his students. In a multicomponent, self-integrated curriculum, total literacy must result from English instruction. A student must receive intensive instruction in the problem phase of his studies without neglecting any of the other components needed for a balanced English curriculum.

Ordinarily, a student who reaches level eight (grade 7) in school is presumed to read well enough to handle the diverse content subjects introduced in the junior high school years. If such a student enters the

[26] David H. Russell, *Children Learn to Read* (New York: Ginn and Company, 1961), p. 261.

level eight English classroom with serious retardation in reading (or any other functional *know-how* skill), he *must receive* instruction appropriate to his case. *New Design* recommends that needed instruction be given without neglecting any of the other functional components in the discipline. The science components should be curtailed (but not omitted) in favor of more art components; the art components should *focus* on the needed skill without neglecting a full range of *know-how* instruction and experience.

Since there is an abundance of literary material useful in teaching the retarded reader, the English teacher should be judicious in selecting materials appropriate to a specific task. It is easy to mar the value of a poem or short story, for example, by using it to develop a higher reading rate or to supply words for a vocabulary test.[27] The problem of language retardation can be solved without perverting literary materials.

LITERATURE AND CREATIVITY

Because the high school student has reached a level of self-conscious intellectual maturity, he needs to respond to literature in ways other than those of spontaneous delight or rejection which were adequate for him as a child, and he needs to know literature on a level higher than a skill-building one. The study of literature *as an art* means that the young student must learn the theoretical principles that comprise the intellectual component of any art; he must learn the variety of forms that verbal artists have often used; he must learn the methods most appropriate to certain forms as well as the strengths and limitations of each method; he must learn what ideas great writers have found worthy of discussion; and he must learn the variety and extensiveness of examples of literary art. Even the retarded reader has a right to this information because it is precisely this which stimulates and frees the creative power of verbal interpretation.

Literary study is important to every student because it develops his creative potential and articulates those values which every adolescent seeks to define. Emerson once said, "One must be an inventor to read well."[28] Every good reader has experienced the pleasure of interpreting through his own mind and emotion the reality that appears before him. John J. DeBoer explains this concept as follows:

[27] The following essay might be useful to beginning teachers: John S. Simmons, "Teaching Levels of Literary Understanding" in Lawrence Hafner, *Improving Reading in Secondary Schools* (New York: The Macmillan Company, 1967), pp. 353-357.
[28] Quoted by Kathleen B. Hester in "Creative Reading: A Neglected Area," *Education*, Vol. 79 (May, 1959), p. 537.

> Creativity in reading differs from creativity in writing, but it
> has in common with it one purpose: to combine and recombine the
> materials of language to produce a meaningful result.[29]

The literature program promotes creativity because it encourages high-order mental processes such as formation of concepts, seeing relationships, making applications, and drawing conclusions. Unfortunately students who are intellectually creative do not always express their ideas well.

Probably the greatest skill of an English teacher is demonstrated by the person who can lead his students to write and speak freely and discerningly about literature. This accomplishment presupposes that the teacher has supplied the methods of worthwhile discussion of literature, the materials, and the motivation as well. Such a teacher shows an understanding of the interrelationships of the language arts and of their influence on the creative behavior of students. The study of literature, if it is to effect the greatest good of which it is capable, must be correlated with *know-how* skills. The science components of literary analysis, literary history, and literary criticism must be made functional so that through integrated study and practice the student comes to see the continuity of man's concern to make meaning out of reality and to express that meaning to others. Though most students cannot create imaginative literature, they can write and speak in response to that literature. They too, though perhaps on a lower order of artistry, are using language as the artist has used it—to formulate, to structure, to integrate, and to express a personal interpretation of reality.

Besides developing a student's power to create, literature also explores the values which youth seeks to define. The yearning and strife which the young adolescent feels can be somewhat relieved by induction into the literature that deals with the human condition. "Perhaps most troubling of all to the young adult is his desire for qualities of sincerity and goodness in human life."[30] Through the broadening social experience he receives through literature, the student sees how other men have come to terms with the problems of life. The vicarious emotional experience afforded by literature also helps him to view his personal feelings in a broader perspective. Finally, the intellectual experience of entertaining the best of what has been thought and said throughout the centuries leaves him with an understanding of the values men have found of lasting worth in life and literature. Walter Loban describes the key function of literature in the transmission of values to students:

[29] John J. DeBoer, "The Concept of Creativity in Reading," *Perspectives on English,* Robert C. Pooley, ed. (New York: Appleton-Century-Crofts, Inc., 1960), p. 199.
[30] G. Robert Carlsen, "Deep Down Beneath, Where I Live," *English Journal,* Vol. XLIII (May, 1954), p. 237.

> A value expresses the essence of experiences the race has found to be worthwhile. Over the centuries, man, guided by the forces of instinct and of intelligence, has groped slowly but steadily toward the humanitarian ideal. The student, in the disciplined forms of literature, discovers these same forces at work; here he finds bared the restless searching human spirit. The literary artist, highlighting now one aspect of experience and now another, is concerned with the mystery of man. Thus literature, embracing as it does the accumulated conscience of the race, provides a medium which allows the student to grapple on his own level with the ideas and values that have guided man in his long struggle from the twilight cave to the light.[31]

With directive skill on the part of the teacher, students absorb human values as they read. *The Revolt of Mother* places the concepts of home and material progress in a challenging perspective; *Macbeth* demonstrates the disastrous results of inordinate ambition; *I Remember Mama* shows the solidity of family relationships; *You Can't Take It With You* stresses the possibility of acquiring a personal integrity that no external circumstance can change; *The Gold Bug* demonstrates human ingenuity; *Under the Lion's Paw* exemplifies the misuse of power; *My Friend Flicka* measures a boy's devotion for a loved one; *The Red Pony* says that when a man's first choices fail him, he must content himself with second best. Thus, by reading, the student grows up into the knowledge and understanding of values men have always prized. Robert Heilman says:

> Books help bring out a potential humanity, lead the individual toward his full status as a human being—in a word, help him to mature or grow up. By growing up, clearly I mean the realizing of certain qualities or attitudes that are potentially present in man but that have to be cultivated if he is to become truly *human*.[32]

The study of literature, then, provides an experience both in personal creativity and in personal valuing. It is here that a youth establishes his identity as a person and as a member of the human family. Dwight Burton says:

> The study of literature must remain at the heart of the English curriculum in the secondary schools, for it is only through a literature-centered program that the course in English retains its identity as a humanistic experience.[33]

[31] Walter Loban, Margaret Ryan, and James R. Squire, *Teaching Language and Literature* (New York: Harcourt, Brace and World, Inc., 1961), p. 603.

[32] Robert B. Heilman, "Literature and Growing Up," *English Journal*, Vol. XLV (September, 1956), p. 307.

[33] Dwight L. Burton, *Literature Study in the High Schools* (New York: Holt, Rinehart and Winston, Inc., 1964), p. v.

The glory of the English curriculum is that it can challenge a student to spiritual growth and aesthetic response. Taught with its counterpart, literary criticism, literature can both delight the student and exercise his powers of judgment and creativity. Integrated with the other components of the language arts program, literature will always emphasize the fact that verbal achievement, whether it be the artist's or the student's, is a unique, personal interpretation of reality.

IV

Public Communication in the Modern English Program

The history of man's oral communication is as old as human society. When men decided to live in groups and solve their problems corporately, the science and art of public communication was born. Speaking to large groups of persons simultaneously, however, was not a unique art; rather it was a development of skill in interpersonal conversation. Until 1450, the date associated with the invention of movable type, men shared their thoughts with large groups of persons in a laborious way: the orator had his voice, and the writer had his pen. In both instances the extent of the communication was limited to the physical power of men. However, with the invention of printing and its later development, the steam-powered printing press, written communication developed a power and extensiveness commensurate with the tireless energy of machinery. The invention of radio, film, and television gave oral communication an ease and efficiency far beyond human expectation.

The history of pedagogy runs a course parallel to the development of public communication. As people began to live in society, children needed training to fit into the prevailing social order. As social living became increasingly complex, children needed increasingly expert instruction in social processes and, specifically, in the medium of social concourse, language. Training its youth to use the available means of communicating efficiently has been a major concern of every age in mankind's development.

MODERN COMMUNICATION AND FORMAL EDUCATION

If the first half of the twentieth century can be called the age of technology, then the last half can be called the age of communication. From the fifties on, Americans have been witnessing an explosion of technological progress, an apogee of technical sophistication in which men talk to machines, machines talk to one another, and machines talk to men. *It is difficult to see how the modern school can ignore the reality of mass media communication, the progeny of modern technology.*

Beyond this unbelievable technical proficiency, there is the universal social reality of *men talking to men* by means of the media. Whether on paper, film, tape, or disc, the content of mass communication will be worthy of the age in which it was born only if it can be integrated with the total culture transmitted to the children of that age. Although schools are generally responsible for the transmission of knowledge, there seems to be little concern by English educators regarding the teaching of the media and content of public communication today. A failure to integrate the new content and media with traditional subject matter in the modern school curriculum has already had serious consequences. For one thing, the English curriculum that perhaps suited students' needs a quarter century ago is alienating the students of today.

Brought up on the visual-aural efficiency of modern communication media, today's children rebel at the limitations of a single print medium. Unless English educators learn to use both the methods and the materials of modern mass communication in the classroom, the school drop-out situation can hardly improve. Children find it difficult to adjust from the immediacy, wonder, and involvement of informal learning from radio, television, and records to the detached verbalization of formal classroom learning. It is easier and more pleasurable for young persons today to create a culture of their own rather than to seek identity and satisfaction through a knowledge of mankind's history of achievement. When the young are allowed to substitute an immediate end for a good which society knows to be more lasting and more beneficial, that society has betrayed its children. Every generation must reassess its cultural heritage in terms of present circumstances, but no generation can afford to cut itself off from the wisdom of the past. The *problem of synthesis* is the problem confronting educators today, especially English educators who are charged with transmitting the humanistic values inherent in man's literary records of communication.

Marshall McLuhan speaks on this point of a need for synthesis:

> Had the Schoolmen with their complex oral culture understood the Gutenberg technology, they could have created a new synthesis of written and oral education, instead of bowing out of the picture and allowing the merely visual page to take over the educational enterprise. The oral Schoolmen did not meet the new visual challenge of print, and the resulting expansion or explosion of Gutenberg technology was in many respects an impoverishment of the culture . . .[1]

[1] Marshall McLuhan, *Understanding Media: The Extensions of Man* (New York: McGraw-Hill Paperbacks, 1966), p. 71.

MASS MEDIA AND ENGLISH IN TODAY'S SCHOOLS

Children today need to learn English *by means of* modern media, and they need to learn something *from the content of* modern communication. Because the print media, the foundation of mass communication through newspapers, periodicals, and paperbacks, is substantially the same as that of literature, *New Design* recommends that all printed material be included under the component called literature in the four-component discipline. Here popular art can be studied as any other verbal art in printed form, subjected to the techniques of literary analysis, literary history, and literary criticism. *New Design* holds that the strength and limitations of the printed media products will best be seen in contrast and comparison with traditional literary subject matter. Under *functional* conventions (a *know-how* component in the English curriculum), students at every educational level should learn how to use modern print media to extend their own verbal art products. As public communication experience, all students should use print media to gain first hand knowledge of the values of these means of sharing ideas with large groups of people. Since there is sufficient precedent in the English curriculum for these kinds of studies and experiences, teachers will have little difficulty integrating new information and content in printed products with traditional content.[2]

Teachers need special imagination to integrate the study of *nonprint media* with existing subject matter in English. The media and the content of movies, radio, television, disc, and tape seem to belong to a special category of sight-sound products. In the new English curriculum, these media are considered extensions of the orator of ancient times. Just as the rhetoric of the speaker in the Roman forum was wholly dependent on visual-aural stimulation of his audience to effect communication, so the new media depend on one or both of these sensory bases. For this reason, *New Design* recommends that mass oral media be designated as an individual component in the English curriculum and be studied as one of the four major constitutents expanded throughout a K-Ph.D. English education.

Delimiting media by the strictures of *mass* and *aural-oral* excludes such technological devices as the telephone and the computer. These do not provide, as yet, for simultaneous communication to large audiences. The stricture of *orality* separates the nonprint from the print media. As academic concern for communication grows, however, a separate discipline of *public communication* will take shape; at that future time, all

---

[2] The value of having elementary, high school, college, and graduate school students create their own newspapers, literary magazines, and paperbacks is generally accepted. *New Design* recommends that these opportunities be an outgrowth of regular classroom instruction rather than projects of highly specialized out-of-class groups.

the public media will share a common fold. Today, however, public communication as a subject of school curriculum is not yet well defined, and the English teacher must make an arbitrary division of subject matter to work efficiently with the *know-that* and *know-how* of an emerging area of English studies. The English teacher bypasses an insistent reality if he ignores the verbal art of the mass media. Charles Steinberg has said:

> For the fact is that we are enveloped in a welter of mass media and we cannot, under any circumstances, exclude them from our senses. The individual and the social group must learn, therefore, to evaluate them properly, use them wisely, and develop their fullest potential in the service of a democratic society.[3]

THE DEVELOPMENT OF ORATORY AS MASS COMMUNICATION

Perhaps if American schools had held fast to the rhetorical tradition originating in Greece and Rome, and transplanted in Colonial America by the British texts of Blair, Whately, and Campbell, the primacy of public communication for free peoples would have been preserved for the present generation. American schools, however, in the great curriculum reorganization of 1910, rejected all classical rhetoric to accommodate the influx of noncollegiate students attending high school. In rejecting the tradition of rhetoric, they rejected both oral and written composition as communication on private and public levels. Neglecting the tradition of oratory meant neglecting a content and pedagogy of public speaking that had received considerable scholarly attention since Greek times.

Because the first medium of oratory was the speaker's voice, pedagogical literature from early Greek times is replete with instructions for maximum vocal effect. The classical masters, Aristotle, Cicero, and Quintilian gave copious instructions on tonal effects, gesturing, and the whole science of public address. (In an earlier rhetoric, Theophrastus did not hand down elaborate rules for effective delivery though his notes on memorization as preparation for delivery were compendious.) It was one of Cicero's contributions to develop instructional materials on the fine points of delivery. In *Ad Herennium* he writes:

> I am not unaware how great a task I have undertaken in trying to express physical movements in words and portray vocal intonations in writing. True, I was not confident that it was possible to treat these matters adequately in writing. Yet neither did I suppose that, if such a treatment were impossible, it would follow

[3] Charles S. Steinberg, ed., *Mass Media and Communication* (New York: Hastings House, Publishers, 1966), p. xiii.

that what I have done here would be useless, for it has been my purpose merely to suggest what ought to be done. The rest I shall leave to practice.[4]

If Cicero can be credited with turning the theory of classical rhetoric into practice, Quintilian should be credited with systematizing a pedagogy of rhetoric. The *Fathers* of the early Christian Church were trained in oratory as well as composition by means of the classical treatises. In medieval times, skill in the public speaking of classroom and pulpit became the hallmark of the great debates and dissertations of the Schoolmen. When Sherry and Peacham published their treatises on figurative language in the sixteenth century, their work reflected a Renaissance interest in the subtleties of language which characterized both the speaking and writing of medieval times.[5] There seemed to be little difference between the intricacies of oral embellishment and the highly figurative language in such works as *Confessio Amantis, The Pearl, Gawain and the Green Knight,* and *Piers Plowman.*

Seventeenth century texts in rhetoric, while emphasizing sometimes the oral and sometimes the written aspect of the art, all seemed united in their common reference to the Bible. Eighteenth century texts were less keyed to the rhetoric of scripture and more concerned with the development of the art of oratory.[6] In this century, it was John Ward, George Campbell, and Hugh Blair whose works were to influence the development of American rhetoric.[7]

It is generally known that in colonial times the early American universities followed the medieval curriculum organization of the *trivium* and *quadrivium.* Thus, undergraduates were trained for at least two years in grammar, rhetoric, and logic as well as in mastery of Greek and Latin. Textbooks used reflected contemporary studies and emphases in seventeenth century British texts.

Because college graduates of the Colonial period were usually destined for the ministry, textbooks used in preparing them were confined to a limited subject field and a limited purpose. One might guess that

[4] Cicero, *Ad Herennium,* Harry Caplan, trans. (Cambridge, Massachusetts: Harvard University Press, 1956), p. 205.

[5] The bibliography of *New Design* lists complete bibliographical data for Richard Sherry (1550) and John Peacham (1577).

[6] For a detailed discussion of the development of rhetoric in England see Mary Nazaire Columbro, *A Conceptual Framework for the Teaching and Supervision of High School English,* unpublished doctoral dissertation, Columbus, Ohio, The Ohio State University, 1964. Primary sources include John Henley, *Speaking and Action,* 1727 and *Defense of Oratory,* 1728; Sir Richard Blackmore, *The Accomplished Preacher,* 1731; John Lawson, *Lectures Concerning Oratory,* 1752; Thomas Sheridan, *Lectures on Elocution,* 1763; Joseph Priestley, *Course of Lectures on Oratory and Criticism,* 1777; John Wilson, *Principles of Elocution,* 1799.

[7] The bibliography of *New Design* lists complete bibliographical data for the works of Ward, Campbell, and Blair.

elegance in oral expression and knowledge of the rhetorical beauties of Sacred Scripture would be the daily fare of early students. Research gives proof of this in Cotton Mather's *Directions for a Candidate of the Ministry:*

> But I will take this opportunity to tell you, that there is no where to be found any such *Rhetoric,* as there is in our *Sacred Scripture.* Even a pagan Longinus himself, will confess, The Sublime, shining in them. There can be nothing so beautiful, or so Affectuous, as the *figures* every where used in them. They are Life. All meer *Humane Flourishes* are but *chaff* to the *Wheat* that is there. Yea, they are an hammer *that breaks the rocks to pieces.* In them the GOD of glory thunders, yea, does it very marvelously! There is in them that *Voice of the Lord* which is full of Majesty.[8]

Research also shows that eloquence was stressed as the main part of rhetoric. *Rhetorica* by Audomarus Talaeus (1510-1562), a book which utilized the selective approach of the Ramus rhetoric (a contemporary text popular at Cambridge), was used at Harvard and Yale. Porter G. Perrin found the following information in his research on rhetoric books in America before 1740:

> Talaeus' *Rhetorica* was certainly current in the colonies. . . . John Harvard's bequest contained a copy, and Increase Mather had one. The closest evidence of use is a copy in the Massachusetts Historical Society having the signature of Dudley Bradstreet, Harvard, 1698, and the date, 1694.[9]

The importance of this information is that these books emphasized one aspect of rhetoric, *pronunciatio,* in the belief that howsoever astute a preacher's sermon content might be, it would be ineffective without excellence of delivery. While Ramus considered rhetoric in general as the third and least important subject in the *trivium,* he nonetheless gave consideration to rhetoric as both expression and action. "Expression included the study of tropes and figures; action dealt with voice and gesture."[10]

Ramean rhetoric, as a matter of fact, was critical of the Aristotelian-Ciceronian tradition. Except in literary allusion, there seems to be little dependency on the old tradition, despite its availability in the same classical languages which the students were mastering. Porter G. Perrin

[8] Ota Thomas, "The Teaching of Rhetoric in the United States during the Classical Period of Education," *A History and Criticism of American Public Address,* Vol. I (New York: McGraw-Hill Book Company, Inc., 1943), p. 86.

[9] Porter G. Perrin, *Text and Reference Books in Rhetoric Before 1750* (Chicago: private edition, distributed by University of Chicago Libraries, 1940), p. 75.

[10] Ota Thomas, *op. cit.,* p. 201. A footnote cites the investigations of Warren Guthrie and Porter G. Perrin as confirming evidence.

offers the following conclusion regarding classical rhetoric in early colonial times:

> But none of the classical rhetoric is given as a text in any of the official programs of study before 1750 and none is referred to by any student still in college in any diary or letter that has been found in making this study. It is of course not safe to conclude from this comparative silence that they were unknown in the seventeenth and early eighteenth centuries. But in view of the facts that other works are mentioned as rhetorical texts in use, that other evidence, particularly the commencement theses, points to a tradition of rhetoric far removed from that of Cicero and Quintilian, and that later, in a quite different academic setting, we find these works definitely in use in the renewal of popular oratory, we may believe that the ancient rhetoricians were in general neglected.[11]

Ota Thomas' research offers the same conclusion:

> Evidence indicates that the classical rhetoricians were largely ignored while the abbreviated rhetorics of Talaeus and Dugard,[12] disciples of Ramus, were widely known and venerated.[13]

One general reason for the antipathy of colonial educators for the ancient rhetoricians might be the fact that the Puritans, men of the later Reformation, were, on principle, in conflict with the Renaissance humanists and their respect for and revivification of the doctrines of pagan antiquity. As American colleges gradually extended their training to prepare men for careers in law and politics, the study of public communication became increasingly important. American textbooks of the eighteenth century matched those of British origin in their emphasis on rhetoric as oratory. Between 1720 and the end of the century, supporting the change from Latin to English as the respected language of the schools, several texts with this special emphasis were introduced. Two important titles are *The Port Royal Art of Speaking* and *The Rhetoric of Oratory*.[14] Until the brush-fire acceptance of Hugh Blair's *Lectures on Rhetoric and Belles Lettres* in 1783, however, the most influential book was Ward's 1759 publication, *A System of Oratory*. This comprehensive synthesis of the Greek and Roman doctrines of rhetoric added the richness of classical rhetoric to the development of public speaking in American schools.

It is a singularly significant fact that Epiphalet Pearson, professor of Hebrew and other Oriental languages at Harvard in 1804, drew up the rules for the administration of the Boylston chair of Rhetoric and Ora-

---

[11] Porter G. Perrin, *op. cit.*, p. 72.
[12] Dugard is an Englishman, 1606-1662, printer and schoolmaster.
[13] Ota Thomas, *op. cit.*, p. 201.
[14] *Ibid.*

tory and based them on Ward's *System of Oratory*.[15] The Boylston chair
(endowed by a Boston merchant in 1772) and the educational prestige of
the Harvard men who have since occupied this post have exerted a distinct influence on American rhetoric, specifically on the separation of
written from oral composition as it exists in schools and colleges today. It
was in 1810 that instruction in English composition (and grammar),
until then given by the professor of Hebrew, became the duty of the
Boylston professor. Had the rules drawn up for the chair been based on
some other less comprehensive system of oratory than Ward's, it is doubt-
ful whether the broad interpretation of rhetoric, governing exercises in
both written and oral English, would have been so firmly established.

Because the rules for lectures and course content were spelled out in
terms of the classical canons of rhetoric and oratory, the first Boylston
professor, John Quincy Adams, in 1806, kept close to the ancients. His
successor, Joseph McKean, continued to emphasize concern for classical
precepts of writing, an emphasis which was to become a rival tradition to
the development of oratory.

In 1819 Edward Tyrrel Channing, editor of the *North American
Review,* accented rhetoric as utilitarian communication, a tradition
which subsequent professors of English often sought to escape. Trained
in German philology, Francis J. Childs could hardly welcome the editorial proof-reading policy bequeathed him by Channing. In 1876 a Chair
of English was created for Childs and he became the founder of the
school of English that Kittredge later made famous.[16]

Adams Sherman Hill in occupying the Boylston chair from 1876 to
1904 not only reiterated the Channing concept of rhetoric as written,
utilitarian discourse, but also advocated a rhetoric based on grammar. It
is this concept which, through the great English curriculum revision of
1910, emerged shorn of the rhetoric which was presumably too *classical*
for the newer democratic educational theories, and glorious in its barren
dedication to *grammar.*

Briefly, the tradition of American rhetoric is one mainstream with
two rival branches, written composition and oratory. Whereas the whole-
ness of the Graeco-Roman tradition, epitomized in the relation of John
Ward's work to the Boylston chair, replaced the earlier nonclassic,
Ramean rhetoric, the rival currents of rhetoric as composition and rhetoric as speech continued to flow strong and independent.

Nineteenth century texts, as well as modern ones, seem to emphasize
without discernible reason sometimes one and sometimes another of the

[15] In "The Boylston Chair of Rhetoric and Oratory," *Western Speech,* Vol. XXIV
(Spring, 1960), p. 85, Paul E. Reid says that Joseph McKean, second Boylston professor,
made this observation.
[16] Paul E. Reid, *op. cit.,* p. 86.

rival traditions. Some early texts perpetuating the rhetoric-as-speech tradition include James Burgh, *The Art of Speaking* (1804); Noah Webster, *An American Selection of Lessons in Reading and Speaking Calculated to Improve the Minds and Refine the Tastes of Youth* (1809); Increase Cooke, *The American Orator; or Elegant Extracts in Prose and Poetry; Comprehending a Diversity of Oratorical Specimens* (1818).[17]

Nineteenth century texts perpetuating the rhetoric-as-writing discipline were also used widely.[18] Authors included Samuel P. Newman (1829), Rufus Nutting (1840), Henry Coppée (1859), Henry N. Day (1850, 1860, and 1867), John F. Genung (1888), J. D. Quackenbos (1896), and Adams Sherman Hill (1897).[19]

Textbooks of the twentieth century show similar disparity between composition and oratory. Too numerous to list, these books, whether for high school or college students, make speech a subject different from written composition. As the century progressed, less and less information from classical sources was used as subject matter in either oral or written composition. Writing texts tended to neglect the *belle lettres* so important in the Ward tradition, repeating the unity-coherence-emphasis trinity of expository prose made famous by Ashley Thorndike, professor of English at Northwestern University, in his 1906 publication, *The Elements of Rhetoric and Composition.*

The diversity implied in the rhetoric-as-speech discipline is perhaps best seen in the editorial policy of *The Quarterly Journal of Speech,* official organ of the Speech Association of America, founded in 1915. Special editors of scholarly repute are assigned to separate departments including American and British Public Address, Drama and Theatre, Homiletics and Preaching, Mass Communication and Opinion, Rhetorical Theory and Criticism, and Phonetics and Linguistics.[20] Scholarly articles on any of these subjects are accepted for publication.

In the secondary schools, the tradition of oratory lost force as the *general education* curriculum became strong. Today special speech classes are available as electives, and expository writing is generally taught as the only rhetoric component in the regular English program. In the colleges, however, the rhetoric-as-speech tradition has developed into various specialties: theatre and dramatic arts, rhetoric and public address, speech pathology and audiology, radio and television broadcasting. As the discipline of public communication gradually defines itself, the

[17] See the bibliography of *New Design* for complete bibliographical data on these texts.

[18] See Mary Nazaire Columbro, "The Development of Rhetoric in America," *op. cit.,* pp. 104-131.

[19] Complete references are furnished in the bibliography of *New Design.*

[20] See cover page in *The Quarterly Journal of Speech,* Vol. XLIX (April, 1963).

oratorical tradition will culminate in the brilliance and efficiency of the mass media of communication: radio, film, and television. Soundtape and videotape will indeed be the extensions of the rhetor who once dreamed of ease and effectiveness in communicating with his fellowmen.

MASS MEDIA AND THE MODERN ENGLISH CURRICULUM

A discussion of the changing conceptualizations of the nature, scope, and function of rhetoric throughout the ages gives the prospective language arts teacher and supervisor an idea of the wealth and flexibility of the rhetorical tradition. Such a discussion should also suggest the appropriateness of fusing public oratory as it was taught in the rhetorical tradition with the methods and content of today's mass media of communication. Such a discussion, furthermore, suggests that the written, print communication in newspapers, periodicals, and paperbacks be studied with other types of literature since it shares a background common to literary art.

New Design in the Teaching of English recommends that the videotape and soundtape media be taught as extensions of public oratory. Today's children at every educational level need some kind of *know-that* information on a phenomenon that pervades their daily lives. *New Design* further recommends that as *functional rhetoric* all kinds of *know-how* information be given to K-Ph.D. students so that they can exercise their individual talent in producing suprapersonal communication by all the means available to man today. Teaching the mass media does not mean, primarily, the adding of factual information about public communication to the English curriculum. It means, rather, examining the content of the media and using the method and circumstance of the media to produce individual public communication. A truly functional rhetoric must include practice in speaking situations as well as in writing situations, if English education is to avoid the embarrassment of producing the Ph.D. graduate who cannot communicate well enough to teach. Exercises in *both* speech and writing are necessary if students are to be trained for democratic living. If discussion is the major means of problem solving in nonviolent societies, where should oral group techniques be practiced except in the English classroom? What has become of the informal debate in the teaching of English? How many teachers are trained to use the panel, the symposium, the dialogue, and the forum as discussion techniques? Where are the tape recorders needed in every classroom for efficient coding of students' verbal production? Why do public address systems in schools become administrative monopolies rather than valuable media of interstudent communication? What happened to the dream of educational television? Where are the portable television units so promising in the training of English teaching personnel?

Students need exercise in handling the *content* of the mass media as well as the media itself. High level integration can be effected when programs viewed at home become the subject matter of other English-related exercises. For example, the key factors in short fiction can be taught as efficiently in relation to television drama as to prose fiction. In class discussions, many students can refer to a variety of programs, thus enriching the English lesson. Children see little relationship between their school subjects and their many hours of television consumption.[21] The English teacher might well serve an important role in helping children synthesize their total verbal experiences by integrating out-of-class popular art with in-class English experiences.

FURTHER IMPLICATIONS FOR THE TEACHING OF ENGLISH

The task of the English teacher is to help the student understand and use the mass media of communication for his growth in total language competency. The Commission on the English Curriculum of the National Council of Teachers of English factors this task down to its component parts and presents a clear picture of what needs to be done:

> Newspapers and magazines, radio and television, theater and film, public forums and public speeches exert a powerful influence on modern life. Young people growing up in the modern world should understand the nature, power, and control of these agencies. They should survey their offerings and be capable of choosing the good rather than the less good among them. They should develop the habit of using these media both for personal enjoyment and recreation and for keeping informed concerning personal and public problems of local, national, and world import.
>
> They should gain the necessary skills in reading, writing, speaking, and listening for using mass modes of communication adequately. They should understand the techniques of propaganda

[21] In May, 1963, the writer surveyed by questionnaire and personal interview 520 students from grades one through twelve in selected public schools of Columbus, Ohio, to determine the bases of discrimination demonstrated by children in their television and magazine selections. This study was approved by E. F. Reichelderfer and Clayton Farrell, director and assistant director of child study, Columbus Board of Education.

In the elementary school group, seventy percent of the children saw no relationship whatever between television programs viewed and school subjects. Another significant fact revealed by the K-12 study was this: teachers ranked fifth and last as an influencing factor in television selection. Only .025% of all the children said teachers influenced their choices.

Detailed results of the survey are included in Mary Nazaire Columbro, "The Role of the Mass Media in the High School English Program," *op. cit.*, pp. 224-261.

and the effect of sponsorship or of personal bias upon the ideas expressed.[22]

The first task of the teacher, then, is to encourage intelligent, individual response to mass communication. If individuality is to be developed, students must be given an opportunity to speak, act, and write their reactions to what is communicated. Abraham Bernstein emphasizes this point in the following remarks:

> Because of the materials that flood from the newspapers, magazines, radio, television, films, and paperbacks, your students can rapidly develop a great big open ear and open mouth, too agape as audience to be active responders.[23]

By encouraging, prodding, and providing opportunities for children to express reactions to what they hear and see, the teacher can help to intellectualize an experience that may have been hardly a conscious one. By expressing reactions to what is seen and heard, children guard against inundation, and sift through the uniqueness of their own personality the meaning and merit of what they take in.

The Commission on English Curriculum recommends that the *who-what-why-on-what-authority* test be applied to commercial mass media communication.[24] This is a valuable approach because it helps the student to apply the standards of authority, truth, and integrity to what he hears and sees. The questions become the student's springboard of creative listening and viewing and of genuine individual response.

This means that the student becomes an active rather than a passive agent in his reception of experience; it means he is an inquirer, a researcher, and a creator. This creativity that teachers foster by encouraging individual response to mass media communication includes all the high-order mental processes: perceiving, forming concepts, seeing relationships, making comparisons, making applications, drawing conclusions.

Abraham Bernstein suggests this kind of critical and creative response when he writes:

> Your students should read newspapers not passively but as active, interacting readers, watchfully, sniffing for propaganda and tendentious editing and mindful of the story's source.[25]

The second broad task for teachers wishing to assist students in coping with commercial mass media is probably more challenging than

---

[22] Commission on the English Curriculum, *An Outline of Desirable Outcomes and Experiences in the Language Arts*, Communication No. 7 (Chicago: National Council of Teachers of English, 1949), p. 4.

[23] Abraham Bernstein, *Teaching English in High School* (New York: Random House, Inc., 1961), p. 314.

[24] The Commission on English Curriculum, *The English Language Arts in the Secondary School* (New York: Appleton-Century-Crofts, Inc., 1956), p. 229.

[25] Abraham Bernstein, *op. cit.*, p. 284.

the first: students must become keen in listening, quick in comprehension, and astute in judgment. Unless a student possesses these skills, the ever-moving kaleidoscope of mass media information leaves him groping at nothing. The power to catch meaning and value is at the base of the entire language arts program. Teachers, who at every grade from kindergarten to college teach the traditional English program well, are, in fact, preparing their students to cope with mass media communication. The Commission on the English Curriculum makes the following assessment of this point:

> It is also essential to note that in considering the media of mass communication, teachers are not really divorcing themselves from the four essential skills around which the curriculum in the language arts revolves. Mass communication modes are not radio or newspapers or television or movies. They are seeing and listening, reading, writing, and speaking adapted to large audience by means of specially devised techniques and mechanisms.[26]

When students in controlled classroom situations are taught to listen attentively to oral reports, teachers' lectures, and class discussions, they are being prepared for alert listening to radio and television. When students are taught to analyze sentences, to determine forms and structures of literary selections, and to note tone, cadence, and rhetorical devices, they are being prepared to handle magazines and newspapers critically. When students are taught to find aesthetic satisfaction in distinguished prose, in inspiring biographies, and in courage, love, and self-sacrifice manifested by characters in literature, they are being prepared to recognize and respond to these human values in movies and television dramas.

Mass media communication is the logical testing ground for those skills presumably taught in the language arts classroom. When it is used in this way it provides a teaching-learning coherence that children need. By making the student's out-of-class experience function as an extension of the instructional center of English, the teacher provides valuable experience in integration which might well serve as a model for the young student.

Ruth Strickland points out the natural unity that exists between English instruction and everyday living:

> Language is so deeply rooted in the whole of human behavior that it is difficult to estimate its function clearly. Any list of goals toward which the school directs its language arts program serves as goals for the entire educational program.[27]

[26] Commission on the English Curriculum, *The English Language Arts* (New York: Appleton-Century-Crofts, Inc., 1952), p. 372
[27] Ruth Strickland, *The Language Arts in the Elementary School* (Boston: D. C. Heath and Company, 1957), p. 437.

Probably the best support of a unified, integrated approach to the teaching of mass media derives from the Loban, Ryan, and Squire assessment of the popular arts:

> The same principles of clarity and purpose apply to communication in the popular arts as to communication elsewhere. Our teaching programs must recognize the students' need to see the integral relationship between many ways of expressing ideas.
>
> Recognition of the importance of a unified approach means that teachers plan no separate programs for instruction in the popular arts; rather it means that experiences in studying and assessing particular achievements will be introduced throughout the six-year program.[28]

By integrating the teaching of the mass media with the traditional English program, teachers can respond systematically and effectively to the challenge posed by the new media. They can, by thorough training in the skill aspects of literature, language, and composition, prepare their students for critical and creative response to commercial mass communication.

MASS MEDIA AND THE TEACHING OF VALUES

When simultaneous communication to vast audiences is facilitated by technological means, the mass media are in operation. Radio, television, motion pictures, newspapers, magazines, and paperbacks are each an individual medium of communication contributing to the end product, the popular arts. In spite of their origin as commercial enterprise, the popular arts can claim a family relationship to the arts as they have been known in Western culture. Thus they serve, to some extent, as the arts have always served: as the embodiment of man's creative spirit, as mirrors of contemporary culture, and as criticism of that culture.

It is because of their limited adequacy in performing the function of true art and true criticism that the products of the mass media cannot be admitted to full membership in the family to which by reason of the commonality of language they ought to belong. Whereas the work of the poet, the painter, the novelist, and indeed every artist bears the distinguishing mark of freedom, divergent thinking, and individuality, much popular art is characterized by sponsor limitations, popular taste, and stereotype. This is easily understood, for in striving to communicate to vast audiences, the media must aim at the common denominator. Divergent thinking is harnessed to public opinion, and uniqueness is fettered to popular demand in a business where success depends on selling-power.

Whether or not the popular arts dramatize the truism that great art

---

[28] Walter Loban, Margaret Ryan, and James R. Squire, *Teaching Language and Literature* (New York: Harcourt, Brace and World, Inc., 1961), p. 387.

must be independent of vested interests is an interesting academic question. However, there can be no questioning the fact that true art transcends *de facto* reality. The popular arts by reason of the kind of art they purport to be are immersed in the *de facto* world which they serve. They are circumscribed by the populace enjoying them.

Walter Loban has made a comment on this point:

> The popular arts are keenly sensitive to the nuances of social opinion. Indeed so readily do the industries respond and appeal to mass interests that they are often accused of cretinizing tastes. In striving for vast audiences they seem to perpetuate the superficialities of our culture.[29]

The popular arts, then, lack in many instances the dimension of true art that transcends things as they are. The commercial mass media are largely committed to entertainment, at best an ephemeral value. It is useless, however, as every experienced teacher knows, to *tell* students about values. Discrimination is a power that grows with exercise in critical thinking conducted under wise guidance. It is the English teacher's task to guide the student's thinking and valuing of *all the verbal realities* that surround him. If a student is to become a truly English educated man, he must be able to make a valid assessment of the value of mass media communication. He must neither disparage its Gargantuan power to inform nor overrate its Herculean power to misrepresent. Both the strengths and the limitations of public communication ought to occupy the critical examination of students at every level from kindergarten to graduate school. Exercise in valuing occurs when students share their reactions, interpretations, and judgments of mass media products with teachers and with one another. By interaction even young students may come to accept the wisdom of Edgar Dale's statement:

> Our almost compulsive search for entertainment is a malady that can both debilitate and destroy. We need entertainment just as we need sleep, but we can have far too much of it . . . We need the meat and potatoes of education.[30]

The fact that students can learn hierarchies of values, however, does not guarantee that the acknowledged *good thing* becomes integrated with their total personality structure. This phase of research in learning has many unanswered questions. For this reason, too, little is known about the *effects* of the nonprint media on videotape and soundtape audiences.[31]

Exercise in valuing means exercise in discrimination, the power to

[29] *Ibid.,* p. 381.

[30] Edgar Dale, "Quotable," *The Nation's Schools,* Vol. 56 (August, 1955), p. 34.

[31] Paul Lazarfeld, "Public Opinion and the Classical Tradition" in Charles Steinberg, ed., *Mass Media and Communication, op. cit.,* pp. 79-93.

perceive and differentiate the qualities of things. Although recognizing quality is fundamentally a cognitive behavior, it is closely allied to man's affective nature. Two different operations are implied in the choice of a good: the intellectual perception of the good quality, and the assigning of a personal hierarchical value to that quality. Because men do not have absolute integrity of personality, being able to know one thing and choose another, they can, in spite of clearly perceiving the excellence of an object, deliberately choose another. Furthermore, any man can prescind from common evaluative judgments and assign a low place in his personal hierarchy for values which are traditionally cherished.

Of course, it is not necessary that men choose always what is best and finest. Indeed such a narrow principle of selectivity would soon unbalance a man's power to cope with reality. Requiring a man to choose always what is best, or what common opinion considers best, contradicts the essential nature and individuality of the person. There can be a hundred factors, frequently unconscious ones, which impel man's choices. There can be as many different concepts of the value of a thing as there are men perceiving that object.

Discrimination, then, as an objective of a single English teacher's endeavor can at best be a vaguely defined goal. A realistic teacher will probably work toward developing power in critical thinking in his students and beware of assigning his own tastes and prejudices as absolute criteria of value. Students are offended when teachers belittle attitudes and feelings (values) which are peculiar to a social group or an individual. English teachers trained in literary appreciation can alienate students or thwart their emotional development by aesthetic snobbery, a disdain for the truths and values communicated by popular art.[32] More can be accomplished by a positive attitude toward all public communication and its indisputable force in reaching out to remind men of their common bonds with mankind. Although public communication does not tend toward the socialization of persons, it does, nonetheless, provide a medium of vicarious social experience. Through analysis and conscious assessment of these experiences, young people can be exercised in valuing that is both genuine and challenging. If the English teacher's responsibility is to transmit the values of man's cultural heritage as they were evident in his verbal artifacts, then it is the English teacher's privilege to structure meaning for students by examining and sampling the values implicit in the content of modern mass communication.

---

[32] Abraham Kaplan, "The Aesthetics of the Popular Arts" in *The Popular Arts, A Critical Reader,* Irving Deer and Harriet A. Deer, eds. (New York: Charles Scribner's Sons, 1967), p. 341.

PUBLIC COMMUNICATION AND THE INTEGRATED CURRICULUM

In a curriculum where cross-component integration is fostered, the teaching of values is simplified. The integration of the oral mass media with the study of literature is useful for purposes of analysis, comparison, proof, and discussion of value categories. Because literature is a stable vertical thread in the K-Ph.D. English education sequence, a comparative study of values communicated by the content of the mass media and the content of literature unifies the student's thinking about values. By reference to a matrix of verbal excellence where a people's traditional values are expressed, present day values show up in clear and meaningful patterns. By appearing and reappearing through the scope and sequence provided in the English program, these values shape the youngster in the likeness of the ideal man he is expected to become.

When teachers plan functional use for *know-that* information about public oratory, videotape communication, and soundtape communication, unity and coherence in thinking about values is strengthened. In functional rhetoric, a *know-how* component, teachers must plan activities in which public communication is practiced by the students themselves. Whether in elementary school or college, the students will strengthen their learning about the content of the subject matter to the extent that they use the behaviors of that area of subject matter. Mass oral communication needs daily practice in group discussion, in public address, and in radio, television, and soundtape broadcasting. Whereas students learn to use the functional conventions of speaking and listening as *know-how* instruction, they need personal experience in using their voices as well as videotape and soundtape media in public communication performances. These performances can be appropriately formal or informal, depending upon the objectives of the English teacher and the educational circumstances of the group involved. The audience will ordinarily be the classroom group in which the students work; sometimes it will be extended groups of students, such as those formed in team teaching situations; occasionally the audience will be the school population; and now and then it will be a large community group.

When students are predisposed for verbal group communication by long experience with the products of radio and television, they find satisfaction and relevance in practicing these behaviors themselves. Public performance, whether at the classroom or community level, creates the further benefit of exercising the student in overt evaluation situations. When a student is involved in the performance of other students or of the commercial mass media, he is in an optimum environment for thinking-feeling response. Whether or not he responds, and the quality level of response, can all be modified by the direct teaching of values, by the demonstrated affective behavior of the English teacher, and by structuring daily opportunities for students to verbalize their evaluative thoughts and feelings.

Just as literary selections form the basis and springboard for student reaction, so, too, mass media selections can stimulate a variety of student response, both oral and written. Writing parodies of commercials presupposes the teaching of those skills needed to discern verbal chicanery. Critical thinking can be encouraged through the writing of television summaries, synopses, and evaluations and through the composing of advertisements, speeches, forecasts, and reviews. Creative talent can be enlisted in writing and producing skits, plays, and television series, and in creating radio scripts, radio panels, symposiums, dialogue forums, and debates.

Thus the teaching of value in mass media communication is a *know-how* element of language arts instruction similar to the teaching of general literary appreciation. By learning and reacting to the ideas contained in the arts he studies and by submitting to the discipline of the forms into which he pours his creative or critical reactions, a student generally comes to know through personal experience the meaning of artistic verbal creation. Individual writing and speaking exercises should constitute a practical, productive, skill-building sequence of study. Forms used by popular artists are singularly valuable to the language arts teacher because they add a refreshing variety and an ever-new challenge to the student. The natural fascination the student feels for his contemporary culture leads him to explore and to experiment with a minimum of tedium those forms that are currently successful on radio, tape, disc, and television. Given opportunities to speak and to write in all literary forms, oratorical as well as literary, students come to appreciate through personal success and failure the meaning of verbal artistry as it has traditionally been practiced in the English speaking world.

In the classroom the student of mass media communication can study anything from the processing of movie film to the details of VHF purchase of the electromagnetic spectrum, according to the resources of faculty, teaching materials, and curriculum objectives. *Know-that* information includes whatever is related to a communication medium itself, whether it be facts of production, distribution, or consumption. Such information, although it is required only to be known and understood, lays the groundwork for the *know-how* skills developed in the overall composition program. When students know the exact number of persons owning television sets and viewing certain programs, they can better understand why Westerns, "cops and robbers," and family situation comedies are the literary stock-in-trade of the television medium. Studying production problems of radio and recording studios, the student can learn the strengths and limitations of each medium and the appropriateness of the oral structures each medium uses to broadcast its message.

Both the content and the forms of the mass media are important to the student's total language competency. The content of the media serves to extend and integrate the student's experience with traditional literary art: today's "cops and robbers" and detective stories can be criticized and evaluated, for example, as extensions of the fifteenth century Robin Hood tales and the Victorian Sherlock Holmes exploits; television fiction can be consumed and enjoyed as popular narrative art that has pleased mankind since ancient times. The forms and factual knowledge of the media buttress the student's concepts and creative power. Knowing the visual limitations of radio, the student can emphasize aural qualities when he writes for this medium; understanding the explicitness of the television screen, the student can criticize and create the drama of psychological intensity; realizing the problems of motion picture photography, the student can discriminate between the mediocre and the excellent in this art. Thus, the *know-that* information in mass media study lays the foundation for genuine *know-how* skill. Mass media study can give the student a command of communication as an applied science, besides extending and integrating his command of communication as a verbal art.

If today's children are to grow in the self-identity and social efficiency related to knowledge and skill in public communication, the school curriculum ought to plan experiences related to these ends. It seems unwise to neglect either the use of modern tape and film or the content of the discipline of public communication in the classroom. The student today has within his grasp the power and effectiveness dreamed of by the orators of ancient Greece and Rome. English teachers can translate this dream into useful speaking skills by focusing the *know-that* and *know-how* information in the English curriculum to the achievement of these ends.

V

Linguistics and the Multicomponent English Curriculum

English linguistics, the scientific study of the English language, is an integral part of a K-Ph.D. English education. Historical facts about the language, geographical information about English language dialects, information on the structure of the language, and various grammatical systems explaining language processes are all interesting information relevant to the needs of both the child and the doctoral student. The young child needs to know the facts about his language because it is the main medium of his sharing experiences; to the extent that he understands factual information about his medium, he gains insight into the complexity and power of the most valuable human resource available to man. The prospective Ph.D. too, whether future teacher, researcher, or author, needs to command the *know-that* aspects of language if he is to see his specialization in its dynamic relationship to the whole field of English studies. The centrality of language both to human experience and to the interpretation of experience argues for close attention to the facts of a language.

DOES THE HIGH SCHOOL STUDENT NEED SCIENTIFIC LANGUAGE INFORMATION?

In terms of achieving *performance* objectives in English instruction, information about language history is needed by *no* student at *any* level of English education. Whatever knowledge is directly related to *producing a verbal artifact* in English must be taught as part of a functional principle. Scientific language information is *know-that* material in the curriculum and is valid for reasons *other than* its usefulness in productive speech or writing.

Scientific language information is necessary for the teaching of *values* related to language. These experiences in valuing include understandings and appreciations like the following: realizing that language changes as a total culture changes; appreciating the fact that grammar is only one aspect of language study; understanding that nonstandard language variations are highly efficient modes of communication to the groups using them; realizing that men are often inadequate in expressing their true selves through language and that they are entitled to considerable compassion in this regard; valuing the scientific method linguists use in collecting, organizing, and describing language data.[1] Although no English student, then, needs *know-that* information about language to *perform* better linguistically, every student needs this factual information if he is to *experience values* related to his native language.

HOW MUCH LINGUISTICS DO STUDENTS NEED?

It is impossible to arrive at measured amounts of any subject matter needed by students at a given educational level. It is the fact that each student is an individual, different in personality structure and cultural orientation, which determines *how much* of a subject he needs. Furthermore, the fact that language experience has little relationship to chronological and educational levels makes the division of language into arbitrary year-by-year courses of study a somewhat suspect practice. The two main criteria for determining how much scientific language information a fourth grader or a graduate student should be taught derive from the cognitive-affective needs of that particular student and from the expectations of the society in which he hopes to gain permanent acceptance.

Because children's cognitive-affective needs and social ambitions are highly individual, it seems logical to suppose that only those persons close to the student will attempt decisions regarding the *quantity* of information needed in particular situations. Of course, groups of students with homogeneous needs and ambitions can be the focus of curricular decisions, but the judgment, if it is to be valid, can be made only by the person who knows the student's needs. This person, in most instances, is the classroom English teacher, the professional person trained to assess the English needs of students. Sometimes parents help directly in arriving at curricular decisions, although cooperative decisions are usually made by curriculum committees made up of school administrators, English supervisors, classroom teachers, and parents. As the child develops more

---

[1] Objectives in the teaching of English that are related to valuing are given considerable emphasis in Arnold Lazarus and Rozanne Knudson, *Selected Objectives for the English Language Arts* (New York: Houghton Mifflin Company, 1967).

and more self-direction, he too functions as an agent in curriculum design by expressing his interests and ambitions.

The question of quantity, then, in the teaching of linquistics has a different answer for different students, depending upon the needs of the particular students and the value orientations of the professional educators, parents, and students involved. It can be said without equivocation, however, that it is impossible to teach values abut language without teaching the scientific data of linguistics.[2]

DO STUDENTS NEED TO KNOW A COMPLETE GRAMMATICAL SYSTEM?

The English language is a vast and complex field of study. No theory of grammar known today pretends to explain the language completely. Except at the level of the graduate specialist in English, there seems to be little reason why a student needs to learn an entire grammatical system as it has been worked out by theorists in the field, whether the system be traditional, structural, transformational, or some other. If a curriculum intends to have students appreciate the structural consistency of the English language, or perhaps understand the creative potential unlocked by syntactical strategies, there is hardly a need to teach an entire grammatical system to achieve these kinds of objectives. *Selected* information can develop the appreciations and understandings appropriate to the elementary or secondary school student.

What needs to be taught are those parts of grammatical systems which particular students need at particular times to make their own verbal interpretations of reality. Information about patterns, transforms, cadences, clauses, and similar facts are related to the student's immediate need *to use* the information in some expressive way. Figure 3 classifies this kind of learning as *functional grammar* and places it with those English components which are related to *ends in production.*

Every English teacher must make an individual judgment (following extensive testing) of what students at a given educational level need to improve their verbal facility. To force students to handle English facts which have no relevance either to their values and ambitions or to their immediate needs to *say something* about reality is to drive them away from formal English education. The integrity of a grammatical system (a suspect quality at best) is hardly a value worth the alienation of children for whom English is a native tongue.

---

[2] In the teaching of values related to English, *New Design* assumes that the teaching act is complete only when the student has personally experienced the value being taught and has interpreted his experience in some verbal mode.

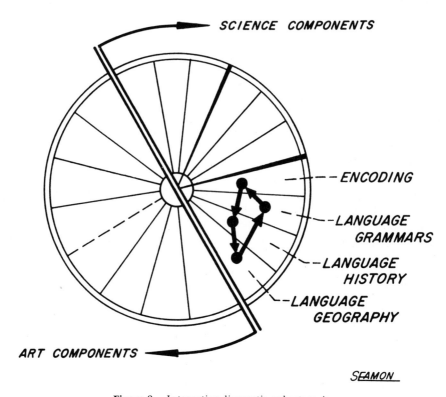

Figure 8. *Integrating linguistic subcategories.*

INTEGRATING LINGUISTICS WITH OTHER ENGLISH COMPONENTS

In language arts instruction linguistics achieves its maximum educative efficiency when integrated with other components. Before describing the relationship of linguistics to other English components, one point must be made clear: linguistics, whether taught as a *know-that* subject or as a *know-how* applied science, must be taught in reference to a *person needing to know*. This is not difficult to do because the unifying substratum of all contemporary linguistic study is its basic concern for language as speech. It is the humanistic orientation of linguistics that makes it a pivotal subject of study for students in K-12 grades.

Linguistics can be integrated in two basic ways: innercomponent or cross-component. When the subcategories of linguistics are integrated with one another, the student learns facts about decoding systems,[3] language history, language geography, and language grammars (traditional, structural, transformational). In these instances the teacher informs the student about particular language data, using whatever historical, geographical, or structural facts he needs to illumine the point and achieve his objectives. Figure 8 shows the four subcategories of linguistics working together. The teacher can also devise strategies in which one of the subcategories is taught in combination with one other. *Ingredients* of a given lesson are determined mainly by the explicit objectives formulated for a particular lesson.

In cross-component integration the student is attending either to *know-that* or *know-how* components. Linguistics can be integrated with literature, mass oral communication, or composition. In combining the scientific *know-that* of linguistics and literature, the *mix* can be made by adding any or all the subcategories of literary analysis, literary history, and literary criticism. Teachers can structure effective English lessons by combining one element of linguistics with mass communication or with composition. Figure 9 shows a variety of cross-component possibilities in the teaching of linguistics. Example A crosses the line separating *know-how* from *know-that* components, combining structural grammar and reading experience. Example B shows how several components, all *know-that* information, might be integrated. Examples C and D show designs for integrating multiple components across the major division line of the English curriculum. These, then, are some model strategies for integrating linguistics with other components in the English discipline.

---

[3] *New Design* uses the term *decoding* to refer to the identification of the basic constituents of a message. Commonly called *reading,* the scientific term *decoding* presupposes *encoding,* its opposite.

See Maria Pei, *Glossary of Linguistic Terminology* (New York: Columbia University Press, 1966), pp. 61, 80.

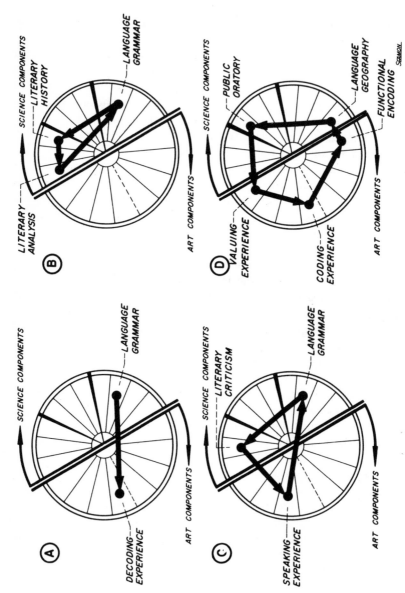

Figure 9. *Integrating linguistics and other English components.*

THE PROBLEM OF SPECIALIZATION

Experienced educators generally accept the fact of precocious specialization; that is, they realize the exceptional ability some students demonstrate for advanced study in a discipline. *New Design,* therefore, recommends that special needs of exceptional children be filled by an intensive study of the English component that interests them. At no time should a balanced program of four major components be neglected, however. Concentration for a limited time should be encouraged because it is by exploring various aspects of verbal interpretation *in depth* that students come to choose an English related college major, a graduate area of concentration, a doctoral specialty, and a life profession.

In the context of *New Design,* specialization must be understood in a particular way. First, English specialization in the broad sense is required of every student in the K-Ph.D. sequence. *New Design* is not a cross-discipline construct. From kindergarten through graduate studies, the student studies only *English* in his English classes. The discipline is presented, however, in a unified way through a four-component self-integrated curriculum. At no time can a student study one of the components of English, excluding the remainder of the discipline. A knowledge of the interrelationships existing among all the components is needed for specialized competency in any one area.

In the context of *New Design,* specialization must also be understood as a study which, while it limits amounts of subject matter, promotes genuine depth in understanding of that limited area. Specialist concentrations are usually arbitrary because fundamentally all knowledge is interrelated. It is for this reason that many Ph.D. programs organize subject matter to be studied so that in one way or another students arrive at a philosophical level of inquiry regarding their specialization. Because a philosopher is generally accepted as a person who investigates reality in its ultimate causes and relationships, the doctoral candidate is encouraged to specialize *to the point where the interrelationships of his subject with other reality become clear.* It is difficult to conceive of an English specialist in literature (*belle lettres*) who is ignorant of linguistic scholarship, who resents journalistic acuity, and who has never written serious prose or poetry. When a man knows his specialty well, he knows the complex interrelationships between his area, the adjutants of that area, and the total construct of knowledge: he must also know how to function as a practitioner of his discipline. In the discipline called English the so-called *specialist* is an imposter unless he knows the fundamental substructure of his discipline, some nonspecialized information about each of the various components, and unless he can demonstrate a modicum of skill in verbal art. In the limited amount of time available for English

studies in a formal education today, few persons are endowed with sufficient intelligence and creativity to master the entire discipline in a
twenty-one or twenty-two year time sequence. The decision, then, to
specialize in the sense of excluding other English components is ill-advised because such a procedure *undercuts* the coherence of the English
discipline which depends for its integrity on the strength of the interrelationships among its various components.

Probably the component most susceptible to separation from the
total English construct is linguistics. Teachers and supervisors applying
the concept of a multicomponent, self-integrated curriculum need to
guard against specialization in language science to the neglect of other
English areas. As popular interest in English swings from one component
to another, English educators must preserve integration and balance for
students in the discipline. The eighteen subclasses of English taught at
spiraling levels of difficulty from nursery school to graduate school provide a wide area of choices by which an educator can provide both
balance and relevance for his students. This concept does not deny specialization to the doctoral student; it insists, however, that all study and
research be pursued in relation to a total English discipline. It also
implies that academic degrees in English be awarded only to persons who
are appropriately knowledgeable in the four components of the discipline
and who demonstrate skill in verbal art. At no level does *New Design*
suggest a rigid or uniform curriculum; on the contrary, it encourages
diversity. The peculiar *mix* taught at any level is the professional decision of the individual classroom teacher.

ENGLISH SPECIALIZATION IN THE JUNIOR COLLEGE

In the junior college or the lower biennium of the four year construct, the English student, regardless of his professional goals, should
receive a complete English education. This can be achieved within the
present structure of diversified courses for levels 13 and 14 in formal
education when the English professor is himself thoroughly grounded in
the discipline he teaches. There seems to be little reason why the freshman composition course and the sophomore period courses should not
continue to teach the total English curriculum found highly relevant to
the needs of high school students. Freshman and sophomore instructors
can present their subject **in focus** as *composition* or *college grammar* or
major British writers or *biography;* in illuminating the pivotal material,
however, the daily lessons will be structured to provide for information
and skills related to the entire English discipline. Figure 10 shows a

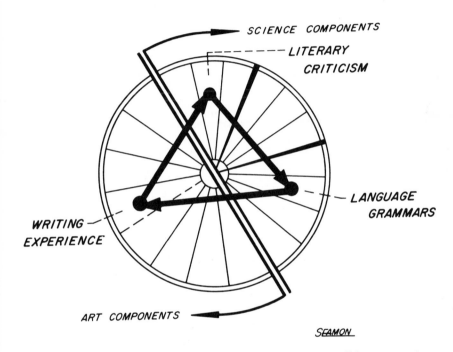

Figure 10. *Integrating freshman composition and other English components.*

strategy for teaching several English components in a single lesson. A practical interpretation of Figure 10 might be an exercise in expository writing (a theme, perhaps), using the critical method of T. S. Eliot's *Tradition and the Individual Talent* on John B. Carroll's essay, "Vectors of Prose Style." In preparing the student to write, an astute teacher would touch such functional components of the English discipline as rhetoric, grammar, and conventions. Thus, literature, linguistics, and composition become the subject matter of a single lesson. An exceptional teacher might also be able to include communication in the strategy suggested in Figure 10 by having the student write a radio speech instead of a theme on the subject.

When day-by-day integration of this kind is achieved in the junior college classroom, the student's conceptual clusters and operational skills related to English become better defined and more meaningful to himself. The foundation for intensive work at levels 15 and 16 is strongly supportive if it has been an integrated entity for fourteen years.

SPECIALIZATION FOR ADVANCED UNDERGRADUATES

By the time a student reaches his junior and senior years of college, he has usually completed his preprofessional or general education courses. Academic course work at levels 15 and 16 is usually organized to support the student's major career choice. In the liberal arts college the English majors at this level are generally future English teachers or students undecided about their careers. Is specialization necessary here?

New Design makes the point that a complete four component curriculum is needed at every educational level from kindergarten to graduate school. It seems unreasonable to distort the English curriculum for future teachers who will themselves be English educators involved in transmitting a multicomponent discipline. Specialization at the advanced undergraduate level should be construed to mean intensive study of separate English components given under such course titles as *Middle English II, Milton and His Times, Literary Criticism, Oral Interpretation,* and others. The liberal arts student without professional orientation can choose freely among course offerings, guided mainly by personal interest. The future teacher, however, should choose courses related to the exigencies of teaching a complete English curriculum at some specified educational level. *New Design* suggests that the pattern of undergraduate choices follow the pattern implicit in the English discipline itself. It especially recommends that courses in linguistics be taken to fill in the language component of the English discipline.

SPECIALIZATION AT THE MASTER'S LEVEL

Whether the young English teacher is enrolled in a Master of Arts in Teaching program (M.A.T.), in a Master of Education (English) program (M.Ed.), in a Master of Arts (English) program (M.A.), or in a nondegree certification program, the basic criterion for selection of course work is the same—its relevance to a total English curriculum. Regardless of departmental regulations for the granting of a particular degree, the young teacher is personally responsible to equip himself to teach a total curriculum. *New Design* argues *against* specialization at the Master's level in some area such as *American literature, Victorian poetry, creative writing,* or *English linguistics.* These areas, while highly relevant to the future teacher, tend to exclude one another in the usual thirty to thirty-six credit hour Master's program. The English teacher who hopes to carry out his academic-professional commitment successfully cannot specialize at the Master's level. In fact, he must often innovate strategies to defeat specialization as it is encouraged, albeit unintentionally, by departments of both English and education.

Such a strategy might be to respond to an assignment by a cross-component investigation. An example might be to fulfill the education professor's assignment to abstract ten research studies by using several studies in linguistics (language), others in literature, some in composition, and a few in communication. Or a term paper on Henry James might concern itself with a transformational analysis of selected narrative passages in *Portrait of a Lady.* In traditionally organized departments where little student initiative and preference in programming is allowed, the graduate student may well be left with no other alternative than to take course work outside his degree program. There seems to be little reason, however, why a combination of English courses, *including courses in linguistics,* should not be organized to give the prospective English teacher both the opportunity to earn his graduate degree and academic experience in the total discipline he will soon be teaching.

SPECIALIZATION AT THE DOCTORAL LEVEL

The integrity of the structure of *New Design* excludes injudicious specialization at the doctoral level. It assumes that the doctoral program in English or English education prepares scholars and teachers for independent academic-professional work which follows the period of formal education. It is difficult to conceptualize an English specialty pursued at the advanced graduate level that does not need a knowledge of the total discipline to buttress related research and practice. When knowledge or skill in a nonrelated specialty is sought, it can be obtained through associated programs or through postdoctoral research and study. There seems to be little need for jeopardizing the integrity of the English program.

There are as many kinds of Ph.D.'s and Ed.D.'s in English as there are possible combinations of courses required for the degrees by various institutions and by doctoral candidates' choices. *New Design* encourages the tailor-made English doctorate, providing, however, that the individual programs reflect the broad philosophical concerns of highly educated men and develop competency in the total discipline. A variety of emphases and course combinations required by individuals to meet their personal needs and professional orientation is recommended; at no time, however, should a doctoral program be organized as an exclusive specialization in only one area of the discipline.[4] Curriculums for the doctoral students have the same design as that of the kindergarten students, except that they support different emphases. Through twenty-two separate yearly growth cycles, the miniature becomes the fully developed structure. The spiraling, year-by-year maturation shows development which can be achieved only when the teaching-learning design accepts the multicomponent content of the English discipline and a recursive method of teaching and learning. If the integrating lines among the components of English have been repeatedly strengthened throughout an individual's English education, he approaches each problem of his academic-professional life with highly developed knowledge and skills. Depth, intensity, and comprehensiveness constitute the English specialty of the man trained in the K-22 English education curriculum.

THE ROLE OF LINGUISTICS IN THE SENIOR HIGH SCHOOL

It is unlikely that an individual teacher will decide to teach a complete grammatical system to a class of high school students. The complexity and comprehensiveness of any one system defeats such an attempt in one year's work. Should a teacher be faced with the problem of teaching a large block of a particular system[5] enjoined by the English syllabus of a particular school, however, some important decisions need to be made. *New Design* recommends that scientific language data be related

[4] Pregraduate specialization for the Ph.D. seems as incongruous with professional aims as pregraduate specialization for the M.D. Can the physician specialize in pathology of the eye without first knowing human circulatory diseases? Can the English scholar-teacher specialize in rhetoric without concern for linguistics, literature, and mass oral communication?

[5] A semester's block of material might be the uses of the noun in traditional grammar, the embedding transforms in transformational grammar, or the technique of immediate constituent analysis in structural grammar.

to the students' need to *use* new information in some meaningful way. Thus, any linguistic subject matter prescribed for a given period of time should be converted into language experiences as soon as possible. This means that the high school student should do more than define, interpret, and explain linguistic facts; he should be exercised in applying his information in some personally meaningful way. In planning daily lessons in linguistics, the teacher must structure modes of student involvement with the subject matter that include affective and physical interaction, as well as cognitive confrontation of the material.

Objectives for such lessons in linguistics should focus on student output. The student is not assumed to *know* the information unless he can *do* something with it. All kinds of expressional activities are appropriate here. Examples include the following: write someone's ordinary speech in phonemic notation; write sentences to match given diagrams, patterns, or transform constructs; debate the merits of some linguistic point; report on a field study into some dialect problem; prepare a taped symposium on the contributions of language scholars to the humanities; dramatize a linguist's problems in handling suprasegmental phonemes.

In this way, *know-that* information becomes *know-how* for the high school student. *New Design in the Teaching of English* recommends that all scientific information in the English discipline, linguistics as well as literary analysis and mass oral communication, be converted into expressed student behaviors, whether those students are in kindergarten or graduate school. The English discipline and the English curriculum are distinct entities for this one fact: the discipline is a structure of knowable facts, the curriculum is a structure of intended behaviors. The curriculum, then, *has been taught* insofar as students demonstrate intended behaviors. These behaviors are the *output* of a teaching system in which the facts of the English discipline constitute the *input,* the instructions of the English teacher constitute the *agent for synthesis,* and the student himself becomes the synthesizer or *performer.*

It is the *performer* in a discipline who adds to its content and life. Every performing student of English is a contributor in the discipline at his own level. A consistent English education will bring to perfection[6] the powers of students to produce verbal interpretations of reality that are meaningful both to society and to themselves. If a total English curriculum has been structured for students already from the primary grades in school, the tenth or twelfth grader comes to his discipline with considerable previous experience. Linguistics, if taught at spiraling levels of challenge from kindergarten to high school, will have myriad interconnections with other components in the discipline by the time the

---

[6] This term might best be modified, perhaps, as *high level working efficiency,* for who is perfect in the English language arts?

student comes to high school. At this level, the classroom teacher must assess the competency, need, and ambition of his students and provide appropriate further development.

Linguistics can be the key to intense language experiences at the high school level if it is allowed to play its full role. The English language of today reflects many centuries of development, and it is interesting and necessary for adolescents to study the medium by which men have expressed their thoughts and feelings and conducted the business of the world for so long. Probably no other segment of the English discipline so effectively gives the student a broad cultural orientation. Albert C. Baugh writes:

> It is not to be expected that everyone should be a philologist or should master the technicalities of linguistic science. But it is reasonable to assume that the liberally educated man should know something of the structure of his language, its position in the world and its relation to other tongues, the wealth of its vocabulary together with the sources from which that vocabulary has been and is being enriched, and in general the great political, social, and cultural influences which have combined to make his language what it is.[7]

Some high school students are ready and capable of studying linguistics as a science. Just as many boys and girls are challenged by physics and chemistry, so too, many are challenged by the unique nature of linguistics which, while maintaining its integrity as a science, functions as a distinctly humanistic enterprise, establishing a line of continuity with the complex social organizations of the past and mankind's extensive cultural accumulations.

Linguistics, then, at the high school level can serve the student's interest in studying a challenging science, or in appreciating the broad cultural values implicit in general language study. At no time, however, should language study be conducted exclusive of literature, communication, and composition in any given year.

LINGUISTICS AND THE CONCEPT OF FUNCTIONALITY

The English teacher at any level of the K-22 language arts continuum must realize that there is considerable confusion in the profession about the concept of functionality. Can linguistics be taught in a functional way? What is functional grammar? Some clarity can be achieved by defining *functional* and relating the term to the basic English construct of *New Design*.

---

[7] Albert C. Baugh, *A History of the English Language* (New York: Appleton-Century-Crofts, Inc., 1957), p. 1.

The word *functional* connotes the idea of performance. In its Latin origin, the root *functio* is the past participle of *fungi,* meaning to perform. Functional grammar has always been construed to mean the elements of grammar a student needs to perform (speak and write) adequately in English. Confusion arises when *functional* is interpreted as *operative* in the discipline and when educators assume that a knowledge of grammar automatically effects language proficiency.

The young English teacher must realize that all knowledge is an abstraction until it is internalized by the student, stimulating his cognitive, affective, and motor processes. All knowledge, then, might be said to be *functional* in that it is an agent stimulating the student to some intellectual-emotional-physical end. Since knowledge does not *necessarily* lead to action of some kind, the teacher's role is to create strategies for achieving that end.

Looking at the complete English curriculum of eighteen separate components in four major categories, it is clear that all the science components must be made functional if the student is to learn them. This is the purpose of laboratories related to science curricula; they are one means of bringing student and abstract information together. Some other means of helping students establish relationships with objective reality (facts in a discipline) include the strategy of structuring speaking, writing, and valuing experiences with these facts. Experience, then, the pressure of performance, effects the *knowing* or learning of a body of facts. The useful art components in the English discipline become a strategy for learning the scientific information.

Looking at Figure 11, however, the English teacher can see that some kinds of information are needed for the execution of a specific task. This information usually concerns procedural principles (*how-to* facts) of which the student is ignorant and needs to know in order to produce an intended result. *The result is not sure knowledge of a body of facts; rather it is the production of some verbal artifact.*

Except for the subject matter of the verbal artifacts, the eight art components of *New Design* constitute a self-contained entity. Facts unrelated to what the student must *produce* can be excluded without jeopardy to the student's output.[8] For this reason, *know-that* information in linguistics, whether language history, language geography, language grammars, or language coding/decoding information, is *not needed* to achieve the objectives of useful art production. There is a considerable body of research and authoritative opinion supporting the *separateness* of science and art components in the English discipline, particularly in the area of linguistics and improved verbal performance.

[8] The converse is not true in the case of science components which depend for the quality of their being known on the intensity of a student's involvement with them.

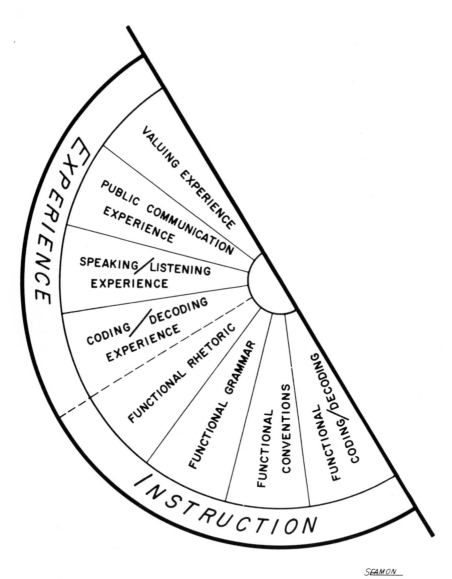

SEAMON

Figure 11. *A complete "know-how" curriculum.*

CORRELATION BETWEEN TRADITIONAL GRAMMAR STUDY AND LANGUAGE IMPROVEMENT

In 1906 Franklin S. Hoyt completed an important experimental study on grammar in the elementary curriculum. Hoyt tested 200 first semester ninth grade pupils from three large cities where grammar was given serious attention in the elementary curriculum. Hoyt found that the operative correlation between grammar and composition was 0.30; between grammar and interpretation, 0.035. In the summary of results and recommendations, Hoyt concluded that

> the same correlation exists between grammar and composition as between grammar and geography; that grammar is of little avail in strengthening one's power to use language; that grammar should be omitted from the elementary school curriculum and left to the high school, or else the character of grammatical instruction should be changed.[9]

In 1926 Matthew W. Willing conducted a study to determine the validity of two procedures for diagnosing the weaknesses of individual high school pupils in the formal elements of written composition. Though neither method, grammar-word tests or single theme writing, was found adequate, the study subsequently showed that students' knowledge of formal grammar had little effect on compositional accuracy. Correlations of the New York Grammar Test with individual written themes averaged 0.43. General language ability, as indexed by the composite of Analogies, Completion, and Word Knowledge tests correlated more highly, 0.80.[10]

In his 1950 article, "Research Concerning Interrelationships Among the Language Arts," A. Sterl Artley writes:

> There is ample evidence to show that there is little if any relationship between a knowledge of formal grammar and English, spoken or written in a functional situation.[11]

As supporting proof of the tenability of his position, Artley cites a number of research studies, some of which include Edmiston, Robert, and Gingerich, "Relation of Factors in English Usage to Composition," *Journal of Educational Research,* Vol. 36 (1942), pp. 269-271; H. A. Greene, "Direct versus Formal Methods in English," *Elementary English Review,* Vol. 14 (1947), pp. 273-285; Walter V. Kaulfers, "Common-Sense in the

---

[9] Franklin D. Hoyt, "The Place of Grammar in the Elementary Curriculum," *Teachers College Record,* Vol. 7 (1906), pp. 1-34.

[10] Matthew H. Willing, *Valid Diagnosis in High School Composition,* Teachers College, Columbia University Contributions to Education, No. 230, 64 pp., (New York: Columbia University Press, 1926).

[11] A. Sterl Artley, "Research Concerning Interrelationships Among the Language Arts," *Elementary English Review,* Vol. 27 (1950), p. 532.

Teaching of Grammar," *Elementary English Review,* Vol. 21 (1944), pp. 168-174.

The Harry Greene study reported the following conclusion:

> The long history of experimental research in transfer of train-
> ing fails almost uniformly to reveal any significant relationship
> between the study of formal grammar and the development of
> skills in English expression.[12]

In his review of pertinent professional literature, Greene noted that from 1900 to 1941 no research evidence had been found to support the teaching of diagraming as an aid to language-composition facility, though this practice prevailed in many schools. In 1941, research by James Reece Stewart[13] showed the following results:

> 1. The learning of capitalization, punctuation, and English usage
> is no more pronounced under the instructional program composed
> largely of diagraming exercises than it was under the one empha-
> sizing composition exercises.

> 2. The diagraming of sentences is no more effective in teaching
> grammar information than is a direct emphasis on composition as
> such.

> 3. Sentence structure is developed as effectively by a composition
> method as it is by the diagraming of sentences.[14]

These results were substantiated in the work of Walter Barnett, 1942,[15] and Claire Butterfield, 1945.[16] These studies upheld Greene's conclusion that a direct method of teaching elements of composition is superior to one expecting a transfer of training from formal grammar to composition.[17]

In 1944 Walter V. Kaulfers, professor of education at the University of Illinois, noted the burdensome terminology of formal grammar. He conceded that it could be taught, but he questioned its carry-over value:

> The point is that no study based on careful experimental
> research has ever shown that such skill, even when attained, makes
> the slightest contribution to the improvement of the individual's
> own personal use of language, either native or foreign.

[12] Harry A. Greene, "Direct versus Formal Methods in English," *Elementary English Review,* Vol. 14 (1947), p. 277.

[13] James Reece Stewart, "The Effect of Diagraming on Certain Skills in English Composition," unpublished doctoral dissertation, University of Iowa, 1941.

[14] Harry A. Greene, *op. cit.,* p. 282.

[15] Walter W. Barnett, "A Study of the Effects of Sentence Diagraming on English Correctness and Silent Reading Ability," unpublished master's thesis, University of Iowa, 1942.

[16] Claire J. Butterfield, "The Effect of a Knowledge of Certain Grammatical Elements on the Acquisition and Retention of Punctuation Skills," unpublished doctoral dissertation, University of Iowa, 1945.

[17] Harry A. Greene, *op. cit.,* p. 285.

In cases involving difficulties in sentence building, the underlying problem is far more psychological than grammatical, that is, the difference lies in the pupil's thought processes and mind-set rather than in words considered as things. . . . Does the remedy, then, lie in superimposing an additional means for promoting insecurity through the introduction of an unwieldy, abstract set of grammatical labels, or of disciplinary gymnastics in the form of sentence analysis, diagraming, or parsing? Hardly.[18]

THE QUESTION OF FUNCTIONAL GRAMMAR

The Shattuck and Barnes work of 1936 gave considerable impetus to the functional grammar movement by stating that formal grammar merited little or no place in the language arts curriculum. Published in the fifth yearbook of the NEA Department of Supervisors and Directors of Instruction, this recommendation received national attention.[19]

At this same time the National Council of Teachers of English in *Conducting Experiences in English* also supported the teaching of functional grammar. Grammar was not to be regarded as a separate phase of the curriculum; it was to be integrated with those skills which carry the burden of expression.[20] Any corrective exercise was to be offered only to those who by test or teacher observation demonstrated a need for remedial work. The new curriculum recommended that grammar be taught not only *for* use but *through* use as well. Grammar was not to be neglected, yet it was to serve an instrumental purpose.

During the thirties and forties, there was no dearth of published material on the principles and practices of functional grammar.[21]

Neither was there a dearth of authoritative opinion from educators favoring functional grammar. W. Wilbur Hatfield, professor of English at Chicago Teachers College and secretary-treasurer of the National Council of Teachers of English for thirty-three years, spared no effort in launching and supporting the teaching of grammar as an instrumental rather than a formal subject matter. As editor of *An Experience Curriculum in English,* he put into viable teaching units the functionalists'

[18] Walter V. Kaulfers, "Common-Sense in the Teaching of Grammar," *Elementary English Review*, Vol. 21 (1944), p. 172.

[19] Marquis Shattuck and Walter Barnes, *The Situation as Regards English* (Washington, D.C.: Department of Supervisors and Directors of Instruction, National Education Association, 1936).

[20] National Council of Teachers of English, *Conducting Experiences in English* (New York: Appleton-Century-Crofts, Inc., 1939), p. 274.

[21] Notable books include the following: Janet R. Aiken, *A New Plan of English Grammar*, (Holt, 1933); Howard Francis Seely, *On Teaching English*, (American Book, 1933); Charles H. Ward, *Grammar for Composition*, (Scott, 1933); Janet R. Aiken, *Common-Sense Grammar*, (Crowell, 1936); Margaret M. Bryant, *A Functional English Grammar*, (Heath, 1945).

philosophy that English is not a body of subject matter to be learned but a series of experiences in which the school offers guidance to insure the child's success.

In conjunction with Walter Barnes, another language scholar, Wilbur Hatfield wrote a section of the ninth yearbook of the NEA Department of Supervisors and Directors of Instruction. In Chapter 2 of the yearbook, he wrote:

> Since language is a social activity, a nexus of habits, attitudes, and skills, it follows that learning language and learning to improve in its use proceed through social activity.[22]

Another educator who championed the teaching of functional grammar was Harry A. Greene, professor of Education and Director of the Bureau of Educational Research and Service at the University of Iowa. Dr. Greene suggested that perhaps the formal approach to grammar had survived because it is easier to set up general subject matter objectives than to identify those skills that genuinely carry the weight of personal language facility.[23]

Lou LaBrant, another educator and author, has consistently favored integration of the language arts skills. Learning should be both casual and practical, she claims.

> The question of how a language program begins may be answered simply. The language program gets under way just as language gets under way at home.[24]

Howard Francis Seely, professor of education at Ohio State University from 1929 to 1958, approved of the new trend toward functional grammar. Critic of the rigorous formality of the older tradition, he wrote, ". . . our teaching of grammar has not to any remarkable extent achieved its purpose of largely and lastingly ameliorating our pupils' language behavior."[25] Deploring an inconsistent and outmoded nomenclature, he wrote in a chapter on grammar:

> I shall close this discussion of the teaching of grammar with a brief plea for the simplification of the terminology employed.[26]

Wilfred J. Eberhart, professor of education at Ohio State University, studied the functional grammar movement. In his doctoral dissertation, "The Teaching of Functional Grammar in the Secondary School," Eberhart discussed the role of grammar in the teaching of English, saying:

---

[22] Wilbur Hatfield and Walter Barnes, "The Situation as Regards English," *A Modern Curriculum in English*, NEA, Department of Supervisors and Directors of Instruction (Washington, D.C.: 1936), p. 28.

[23] Harry A. Greene, *op. cit.*

[24] Lou LaBrant, *A Modern English Curriculum, op. cit.*, p. 31.

[25] Howard Francis Seely, *On Teaching English* (New York: American Book Company, 1933), p. 20.

[26] *Ibid.*, p. 79.

> It is, moreover, extremely doubtful whether the study of grammar can make a vital contribution to the power of building clear, vigorous, and varied sentences, desirable though this end is. The real function of such study is much more *correctness* of expression, as distinguished from *effectiveness* of expression.[27]

This definition of functionality closely follows that of Harry Rivlin, who said that *functional* was "that application of the knowledge of a grammatical item which will prevent the commission of an error in English or will assist in the correction of an error already made.[28]

In 1960, Searles and Carlsen summarized efforts the functionalists had made in the preceding two decades to make grammar relevant to the students' need to produce verbal art.

> Repeated appeals have been made for a reduction in the amount of formal grammar taught; for practice rather than theory, especially in the elementary school; for emphasis on those grammatical concepts which are demonstrably useful in improving the language skills of students; and for the abandonment of grammatical analysis as a means of teaching standard usage.[29]

Still more specifically, Henry C. Meckel summarizes the results of research which supported the functional grammar movement:

> Reviews of educational research, however, have continually emphasized that instruction in grammar has little effect upon the written language skills of pupils. The interpretations and curricular applications of this general conclusion have ranged from the view that grammar and usage should not be taught in isolation to the position that formal grammar merits little or no place in the language arts curriculum.[30]

THE NEW GRAMMARS AND VERBAL FACILITY

Until 1960, all research studies investigating the relationship of grammar to verbal production used *traditional* grammar. Since 1960 every English language study, except one, concerned itself with an analysis of students' language *freely produced*.[31] By 1967, no study except that

---

[27] Wilfred J. Eberhart, "The Teaching of Functional Grammar in the Secondary School," unpublished doctoral dissertation, The Ohio State University, 1936, p. 41.

[28] Harry N. Rivlin, "Functional Grammar," unpublished doctoral dissertation, Teachers College, Columbia University, No. 435, 1930, in Harry A. Greene, *op. cit.*, p. 277.

[29] John R. Searles and G. Robert Carlsen, "Language, Grammar, and Composition," *Encyclopedia of Educational Research*, Chester W. Harris, ed., American Educational Research Association (New York: Macmillan Company, 1960), pp. 454-470.

[30] Henry C. Meckel, "Research on Teaching Composition and Literature," *Handbook of Research on Teaching*, N. L. Gage, ed., American Educational Research Association (Chicago: Rand McNally and Company, 1963), pp. 966-1006.

[31] See bibliographical listings for *structural* analysis of freely produced children's language: Loban, Strickland, Hocker, Riling, Sam, and Stine. See Menyuk, Hunt, Slobin, and O'Donnell for *transformational* analyses.

of Donald Bateman and Frank Zidonis reported on the relationship between the *teaching* of a new grammar and the students' verbal behavior.[32] Bateman and Zidonis compared the in-class writing of two groups of children (for two consecutive years), one group receiving no formal instruction in grammar, the other studying transformational grammar. By means of an index of transforms, the investigators arrived at a structural complexity score for the writing of students involved in the study. The key conclusion of the study was stated as follows:

> Statistical analysis suggests, but does not prove, that there is a relation between a knowledge of generative grammar and an ability to produce well-formed sentences of greater structural complexity. Because the experimental subjects increased the average complexity scores in *well-formed sentences* to a greater degree than did the control subjects, and because the control subjects increased the average complexity scores in *malformed sentences* to a greater degree than did the experimental subjects, there is a strong inference that it was the knowledge of the generative grammar that enabled the experimental subjects to increase the complexity without sacrificing the grammaticality of their sentences.[33]

The English teaching profession is generally aware of the fact, then, that traditional and functional grammar did not improve students' language performance to any appreciable extent. Nor could a new grammar, transformational, claim any correlation beyond a 0.05 statistical level of significance. Research in both areas, however, has been eminently successful in bringing the profession to face the foundational question of *how to teach* children to improve their verbal art.

New Design is explicit in stating that English students at every educational level need to study the grammar of their language under the aspect of *functionality.* Since *functional grammar,* in the history of English pedagogy, has referred to a particular movement related to grammatical correctness, a better term might be *functioning grammar. New Design,* however, uses the term with confidence that the novice teacher has understood that it is impossible to improve children's verbal performance without supplying appropriate *know-how* instructions. It is, perhaps, the peculiar genius of the Bateman-Zidonis research study that it has identified and systematized a body of grammatical rules (transforms) from the vast theoretical field of transformational-generative grammar which students found *useful* in expressing their ideas. Adapted to student needs at various levels, this new *functional grammar* promises

---

[32] Donald Bateman and Frank J. Zidonis, *The Effect of a Study of Transformational Grammar on the Writing of Ninth and Tenth Graders* (Champaign, Illinois: National Council of Teachers of English, 1966).

[33] *Ibid.,* p. 39.

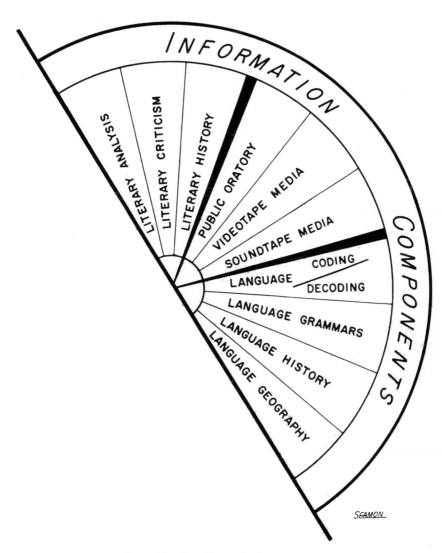

Figure 12. *Ten "know-that" components.*

to improve not only correctness but effectiveness as well. The transform rules stated in mathematically precise language constitute a logically inviolable set of instructions for teachers to give to students who need them. See Figure 11 to note how a functional grammar coupled with a functional rhetoric and with lessons in coding and conventions is sufficient instructional material to develop the student's compositional competence. Provided the student is given sufficient *experience* in using his *instructions,* that is, in actual reading/writing, speaking/listening, public communication, and valuing, he *does not immediately need* the factual information of the *know-that* scientific components in the English discipline. See Figure 12 to note that the ten information components in an English curriculum can be considered a different kind of component, suitable for aims different than a student's immediate need for instruction and experience in making meaning out of reality.

The information components serve as a body of enrichment to the English student. According to the integrative pattern of *New Design* they are the subject matter of the student's planned experiences in English. Depending on the needs of particular students and the educational philosophies of curriculum makers, the experiences in scientific *know-that* information will vary in breadth and intensity. Ordinarily they are highly relevant to the needs of American youth educated to live in a humanistic, democratic society. The information components are, in fact, the *experiences* other English educated men have had in making verbal interpretations of reality. Scholars know that any discipline is a self-perpetuating entity. In the construct of *New Design,* the student is given the subject matter, the instruction, and the experience in making verbal meaning out of reality. He needs only the motive and the talent to make a singular contribution to the discipline in which he was trained as others before him were trained to create verbal art products.

Linguistics, the experience men have had in working with language, is an enrichment area to any student in the discipline. It stimulates appreciations, interpretations, definitions, classifications, indeed, all cognitive and affective responses. It is an information category, however, and detailed linguistic methods as well as entire grammatical systems have little relationship to every person's need to make continuing verbal interpretations of reality. If the teaching of formal grammar in the classroom has failed to help students write and speak better, this is the reason: students do not need to know the niceties of academic systems. Traditional grammar in its effort to analyze a highly complex phenomenon, human utterance, is a formidable body of knowledge. School grammars erred in trying to maintain the integrity of the system in their pedagogical adaptations. The amount of subject matter necessitated artificial segmentation and sequence, a practice which defeated even accidental usefulness, since language *functions* all at once.

If the teaching of structural grammar, transformational grammar, or some other grammar succeeds in helping students speak and write better, it will be because the *theory of the grammar* will be taught as *enriching information* while *useful parts of the grammar* will be related to the students' urgent need *to use language efficiently*. The transformational grammar taught in the Bateman-Zidonis study to ninth and tenth graders never pretended to be the systematic study of the grammar of Chomsky, Lees, Fillmore, and others. It is rather a *pedagogical adaptation* of facts from a theory of grammar which is functionally related to what students must do to express themselves effectively.

Any new grammar, then, that enters the English corpus offers potential enrichment to English students. The question of which students at which educational levels need the grammar is one requiring curriculum decisions at local levels. One fact is plain: the system in its entirety is not relevant to the student who needs a *total English education*. Furthermore, the system-in-fragments cannot function effectively. Any new grammar also offers potential for a *functional* grammar, a microsystem that can be taught in a single academic level, one stripped of all information except *instructional* rules for producing effective utterances.

HISTORICAL DEVELOPMENT OF ENGLISH GRAMMAR STUDY

A knowledge of the history of various English grammars will help teachers make correct decisions about informational and instructional aspects of linguistics.[34] Since there is considerable material available on this aspect of language, a brief discussion here will serve the purpose of showing how language scholarship precipitated a cleavage between the science components and the art components of the English curriculum.

The origin of Western scholarship in language was in Greece where philosophers sought to describe the nature of human discourse. Even here, two groups of investigators were evident, those interested from a purely philosophical point of view (knowing the *truth* about the reality called language) and those interested in systematizing a body of information for pedagogical purposes. The ends-in-itself group, men concerned with philosophic-scientific matters such as the source of verbal compe-

[34] See H. A. Gleason, Jr., *Linguistics and English Grammar* (New York: Holt, Rinehart and Winston, Inc., 1965) pp. 3-87, for a detailed overview of the origins of modern linguistics. See also John Thomas Waterman, *Perspectives in Linguistics* (Chicago: University of Chicago Press, 1963). A further resource is Francis Dinneen, S.J., *An Introduction to General Linguistics* (New York: Holt, Rinehart and Winston, Inc., 1966).

tence, originated what was to become a long *tradition* of *know-that* information in linguistic study. The ends-in-production group, men concerned with the pedagogical implications of theoretical investigation, began a separate development of *know-how* information that was to survive as *school grammar.*

School grammar, then, had its roots in the pedagogical literature of Greece and Rome. Dionysius Thrax (second century B.C.) and Appolonius Dyscolus (second century A.D.) are credited with defining and classifying the parts of speech of Greek and Latin. Students throughout the Middle Ages, the Renaissance, and Elizabethan times, used prescriptive school grammars to translate works from one language to another. In 1762 when Robert Lowth, Bishop of London and professor of poetry at Oxford University, published *A Short Introduction to English Grammar,* his prescriptions for purity and diction and correctness of grammar were a milestone in the continuing development of school grammar. Organized to serve a practical end, acceptable verbal artifacts, school grammar (ancient, medieval, and modern) preserved its identity as a tool subject. Until modern times, its justification for classroom use was its utility in translating from one language (usually Latin) to another. Later it was assumed to have the same utility in guiding verbal production in English for native speakers.

As American research studies from 1906 to 1945 gradually accumulated to disprove any significant correlation between a knowledge of school grammar and a child's verbal behavior, an adaptation of school grammar, *functional* grammar, became popular. The realistic approach of the functional grammarians insisted that the student was not doing language translations and therefore needed to know few of the grammatical intricacies developed through centuries of grammar scholarship and pedagogy. Functional grammarians said that the student should learn only those grammatical items which were useful to him in achieving correct English usage; detailed grammatical analysis should be abandoned; and language learning should proceed through social activity.

Traditional grammar, the broad field of linguistic study with a philosophic-scientific orientation different from pedagogical grammar, maintained a continuous line of development throughout the history of Western scholarship. Following the speculations of Greek philosophers on the nature of language, the early fathers of the Christian church were vitally concerned with the correspondence of language and thought, especially in doctrinal matters. The scholasticism of the Middle Ages supported theories and investigations regarding the relationship of philosophy and logic. During the Renaissance and the following period of great explorations, the revival of interest in the classical past and non-European language grammars developed. Sanskrit, Syriac, and Arabic became the standard languages of comparison with Latin and English, and opened up a whole new line of activity in comparative, historical, and descriptive linguistics abroad. England transported both academic linguistics and pedagogical grammar in the treatises on language and grammar texts it brought to the New World.

Two new developments in linguistics, structural and transformational theory, have been wholly American phenomena. Each is particularly interesting because (while it developed a relationship with the great tradition of language scholarship) it was also able to develop a counterpart in pedagogical grammar. Structural and transformational grammar, then, have been systematized both as conceptual explanations of English language events and as pedagogical systems useful to school children.

In the structuralist group, Franz Boas, professor of anthropology at Columbia University (1899) is credited with pioneer success in the field methods and descriptive techniques now associated with structural linguistics. Some of his followers include Edward Sapir, Leonard Bloomfield, George Trager, Henry Lee Smith, James Sledd, Albert Marckwardt, Nelson Francis, H. A. Gleason, Jr., Archibald Hill, Charles Hockett, Charles Carpenter Fries, and others.

It is important to note that several structural linguists became interested in the pedagogical implications of their new system of language study. Supported by the efficiency of mass media communication, Charles Carpenter Fries (*American English Grammar*) and Trager and Smith (*An Outline of English Structure*)[35] were able to show English educators the ends-in-production values of the new grammar. When Paul Roberts, a schoolman, published *Patterns of English*[36] as a high school text in structural grammar, the English teacher had a working classroom synthesis of structural grammar. Recently, the National Council of Teachers of English has published several adaptations of structural grammar for the high school level. Commercial publishing houses (some in consultation with linguists) have brought out a variety of workbooks, textbooks, films, reading programs, filmstrips, and records for teachers' use in the classroom.

In the transformational group of academic linguists, Noam Chomsky, pupil of Zelig Harris, a structuralist, is credited with developing the seminal theory of transformational-generative grammar. The publication of *Syntactic Structures*[37] in 1957 stimulated unprecedented discussion and controversy and an ever increasing number of related studies. Theorists in transformational-generative grammar include Rob-

[35] The bibliography of *New Design* gives complete publishing data.
[36] See bibliography.
[37] See bibliography to *New Design*.

ert B. Lees, Charles J. Fillmore, Neal F. Johnson, and others.[38] Schoolmen successful in adapting the new theory to *ends-in-production* use for
the classroom include Paul Roberts, Donald Bateman, and Frank
Zidonis.[39] Paula Menyuk, Kellogg Hunt, Roy O'Donnell, Donald
Bateman, and Frank Zidonis have published results of research studies in
which they used an index of transforms to determine the grammatical
complexity of children's writing.[40]

The great tradition of language scholarship, then, continues vigorous and unbroken from Greek times to the present day. Parallel with the
tradition of scientific linguistics, school grammar maintains its own development as a pedagogical tool. If and when other theories of grammar
are accepted in language scholarship, school grammar will once more
reshape itself in the light of new knowledge. The task of the English
education scholar is precisely this, to recreate new knowledge in his discipline in terms of its relevance to students in a K-Ph.D. learning construct.
The English education *language* scholar today is watching the development of transformational grammar, waiting for a definition of the
suprasegmental system operative beyond the syntactical level. Because it
will be some time before a complete working definition of the English
language will be available for classroom use, it may be that synthetic
grammars, pedagogical syntheses of several grammatical systems, will
prove most efficient in the classroom for the present. English education
language scholars are presently creating and testing a variety of hybrids
in experimental situations, conscious of the fact that any synthetic system
must be open-ended to allow for inclusion of new knowledge.

If transformational grammar can prove its claim to be a model of the
psychological process of sentence formation, and if useful adaptations of
the system can be used in school to produce better verbal behavior, this
grammar will gradually take precedence over all others. At no time,
however, should the commitment of an English educator exclude the diverse and unpredictable needs of students in favor of the beauty of a
system. In the direct application of any truly functional grammar, the
classroom teacher must decide what particular students need to know to
produce improved verbal interpretations of reality. If an appreciation for
the specificity of a system, its consistency, its psychological validity, or
some similar value is intended as an objective of instruction, then the
grammar, however much it pretends to be a *school grammar,* becomes
scientific *know-that* information, exclusive of the production needs of
students.

A brief survey of the historical development of linguistics, then, shows

[38] See bibliographical notation.
[39] See bibliographical references.
[40] See bibliography.

two parallel traditions, the nonschool, philosophical, language research studies and the pedagogical, language learning adaptations. Educators have not always been aware in which tradition their curriculum selections have been. *New Design* places the nonschool grammars with other scientific *know-that* components of the English discipline; it places pedagogical grammar with the *functional know-how* components of the discipline. *New Design* notes that school grammars of the past have failed to effect improved verbal production in students because the grammars were taught as *scientific know-that* instead of *functional know-how*. *New Design* also notes that new grammatical theories must be adapted and tested for relevance to the actual needs of K-Ph.D. students before they are implemented in English curriculums as truly *functioning* grammars.

In view of this knowledge, the English teacher should remember that grammar is not the whole of linguistics; the complex system of encoding and reading, the history of language (both diacronic and synchronic development), and linguistic geography are also subcategories of scientific language study. The teacher should also note that functional grammar is a priority in the English curriculum, and that instruction in *know-that* information should not supplant *know-how* instruction until the student has achieved normative standards in verbal interpretation. The teacher should further note that the ultimate curriculum decisions about what *actually functions* with particular students is his, and that it is his responsibility to shape the discipline to the needs of particular individuals, without destroying its integrity. Finally, the English teacher might help to clarify confusion in the profession by using the term *linguistics* in reference to the nonschool, philosophic-scientific body of knowledge related to an understanding of language, and by using the term *grammar* to designate the pedagogical adaptations of linguistic information which students need to improve their verbal production.

VI

The Role of Rhetoric in a Self-Integrated Discipline

Man's struggle to establish consonance between himself and the world around him is an ancient one. Runes, hieroglyphics, pictographs, manuscripts, books, films, and electronic tapes all testify to man's long preoccupation with self-representation through verbal symbol. The art underlying man's expression of *self-ness* is the art of rhetoric. As man interacts with reality and struggles to interpret his expression verbally, he uses the art of rhetoric to communicate his experiences to his fellow man. Because rhetoric as an intellectual discipline follows the rules of inner speech that characterize self-conscious human activity, the use of rhetoric in composing verbal interpretations of reality enhances the intelligibility of communication. A study of rhetoric emphasizes the personal, creative quality of all verbal discourse.

Although a generative grammar seeks to explain the human capacity to make intelligible predications about reality at the one-sentence, syntactical level, it is the science and art of rhetoric that has traditionally been concerned with explaining the interrelationships of statements in the structure of discourse. Man needs to use the wide creative resources of language to develop his humanity and to join the mainstream of human concerns and aspirations. In developing his human powers of verbal interpretation, each person becomes aware of the uniformity of human nature and the virtually identical powers all men share in giving meaning to reality.[1] In striving for maximum effectiveness in verbal art, men have looked for factual information and *know-how* instruction in the discipline called rhetoric.

[1] Noam Chomsky, *Cartesian Linguistics* (New York: Harper and Row, Publishers, 1966), p. 71.

WHO NEEDS TO STUDY RHETORIC?

Both modern and classical rhetoricians agree that a discipline like rhetoric, one closely allied to thought processes, is universally practical. Karl Wallace suggests that the whole art of rhetoric, both writing and speaking, would revivify the teaching of English at any instructional level.[2] Albert Kitzhaber recommends that logic, rhetoric, and language be the basic components of courses in English for college freshmen.[3] Aristotle held that rhetoric was a counterpart of dialectic, saying:

> . . . both have to do with matters that are in a manner within the cognizance of all men and not confined to any special science. Hence all men in a manner have a share of both; for all, up to a certain point, endeavor to criticize or uphold an argument, to defend themselves, or to accuse.[4]

Quintilian recommended that children (boys) begin to study rhetoric at the age of seven, since by this time they had learned to read. His reason for urging rhetorical instruction early was that there should be sufficient time to develop proficiency through practice. "No man can be an orator untaught," he said.[5]

It seems that rhetoric from its origin has been consistently defined as an art with implicit utility. Within the construct of *New Design,* theoretical information about the forms of public oratory, the historical development, purposes, and procedures related to each form, the arguments for using one form rather than another for specific occasions, and similar technical information is included in the *science* category of components. Along with radio and film broadcasting, public speaking is one of three subdivisions of the mass oral communication component. As *know-that* information, public speaking has the same interest for students in the K-Ph.D. learning sequence as does literature and linguistics. There is a sizeable body of knowledge available for adaptation to classroom use at any instructional level. The topics of style and delivery, for example, have received centuries of oratorical criticism. Already in Quintilian's times there was the problem of selectivity in *which* subject matter to teach as scientific *know-that* information. Quintilian wrote:

> It is true that writers on rhetoric have, by the pertinacity with which they have defended their opinion, made the principles of the science which they profess somewhat complicated; but these

[2] Karl R. Wallace, "Towards a Rationale for Teachers of Writing and Speaking," *English Journal,* Vol. L (September, 1961), pp. 384-391.

[3] Albert Kitzhaber, *Themes, Theories, and Therapy: The Teaching of Writing in College* (New York: McGraw-Hill Book Company, Inc. 1963).

[4] Aristotle, *The Art of Rhetoric,* John Henry Freese, trans. (Cambridge, Massachusetts: Harvard University Press, 1959), p. 3.

[5] Quintilian, *Institutio Oratoria,* Vol. I, H. E. Butler, trans. (Cambridge, Massachusetts: Harvard University Press, 1959), p. 332.

principles are in reality neither obscure nor hard to understand. Consequently, if we regard the treatment of the art as a whole, it is harder to decide what we should teach than to teach it.[6]

Rhetoric as a useful art, as *know-how* information, is similarly rich in subject matter. Information, both classical and modern, is usually presented as instructions or explanations of how to proceed in speaking or writing to attain a desired end. According to *New Design* this aspect of the major component of composition is called *functional rhetoric*. The term *functional* clearly shows that teaching will concern itself with giving instructions to the student on *how to* invent, arrange, compose, and present a rhetorical piece. In the elementary and junior high school, depending on the ability and experience of the students, some work relating to the history and criticism of public oratory will be begun. This is best accomplished by integrating the *know-how* of functional rhetoric with the *know-that* of scientific rhetorical information. The subject of children's writing and speaking might be, for example, information about the way Greek and Roman boys learned their language arts. The forms used for oral and written experiences might be, for example, those long-honored in the discipline of oratory—the symposium, the dialogue form, the eulogy, the debate.[7]

As students become more proficient in using rhetorical forms and information, there will be less emphasis on the functional and experimental components and more on scientific, theoretical components. One kind of component does not exclude the other at any educational level, however. It is at the teacher's discretion whether fifth grade boys, for example, might profit from a three-day unit on the mechanics of radio broadcasting, or whether a group of graduate interns needs continuing experience in using the basic discussion techniques.

Because rhetoric, like grammar, touches an infinitely perfectible human skill, man's power to communicate his thoughts, it will always be eminently useful at every level of the K-Ph.D. sequence in English education. There seems to be little value in arguing that by definition rhetoric is concerned with forensic speaking, with political and legal debate. The classicists contended long and thoroughly on the problem of defining rhetoric, but none denied that its glory was in the practical end of training someone to perform in a verbally persuasive way.[8] Quintilian cham-

[6] Quintilian, *Institutio Oratoria*, Vol. III, H. E. Butler, trans. (Cambridge, Massachusetts: Harvard University, 1959), p. 179.

[7] *New Design* recommends that reports children prepare be shaped to specific forms. As in literature, so in oratory, form is intrinsic to meaning and purpose. Learning is enriched when children are taught to use traditional forms. Such knowledge and experience becomes the base for creative divergence.

[8] There is a clear discussion of this problem in Donald C. Bryant, "Rhetoric. Its Functions, and Its Scope," *Quarterly Journal of Speech*, Vol. 39 (December, 1953), pp. 401-424.

pioned the broad application of rhetoric as *the science and art of speaking well,* without limitation as to the subject matter of the discourse or the occasion of the talk.

TWO RHETORICAL TRADITIONS

Just as the development of linguistics encompassed two kinds of investigations, philosophical-theoretical linguistics and applied school grammar, so too the development of rhetoric encompassed a speculative-theoretical body of knowledge and a practical, applied school rhetoric. At no time, however, were the studies far removed from one another. The character of rhetoric as a *function* of *language* pervaded both theoretical and practical exegeses. A glimpse of the history of rhetoric will show that the *know-that* and *know-how* aspects of the discipline developed side by side.

Although the birthplace of rhetoric as a practical art is generally designated as the island of Sicily where Corax and Tisias won fame in 469 B.C. by helping property litigants against the state, it was the island of Greece which was to anchor the development of its long tradition as a theoretical science. Names such as Gorgias, Agathon, Polus, Licymnius, Evenos, Alcidamas, Polycrates, Thrasymachus, Protagoras, Hippias, Theodorus, Isocrates, and Theodectes are prominent in the early development of rhetoric, and probably none is more celebrated than that of Plato. Two Platonic dialogues, *The Gorgias* and *The Phaedrus,* discuss the subject of rhetoric, but they are concerned with the nature and scope of rhetoric rather than its utility. *The Phaedrus* presents a philosophical theory of what rhetoric ought to be if it is to justify its claim to be a true art. It is here that Plato defines the art:

> Rhetoric is the art of winning [arguments] by discourse, arguments not only in the courts of justice and public councils but in private conferences as well.[9]

In his characteristic whittling down of several proposed definitions, Plato arrives at the negative conclusion that rhetoric is a false art, an artifice of persuasion by which the unintelligent can be led to beliefs beyond their knowledge. When Socrates himself is asked to give his definition of rhetoric, he replies that it is a fake art, a kind of flattery that simply gratifies and pleases the hearer. Socrates himself left no written texts.[10]

The tradition of rhetoric as philosophical inquiry is difficult to keep

[9] Plato, *The Phaedrus,* W. C. Helmbold and W. G. Rabinowitz, trans. (Indianapolis, Indiana: Liberal Arts Press, Bobbs-Merrill Company, 1958), p. 48.
[10] Quintilian, *Institutio Oratoria,* IV, Books X-XII, *op. cit.,* p. 247.

distinct from practical rhetoric because a philosophical good, happiness (Aristotle), was construed to be the object of the discipline. Moral purpose, the ethos of the speaker, and the emotions of an audience all were an integral part of a *practical* rhetoric. Furthermore, in classical times the scholar-philosopher was also a teacher, concerned about the communication of his specialty to his disciples. Thus, Tisias was the pupil of Corax; Gorgias, Isocrates, and Lycias were pupils of Tisias; Agathon, Polus, Licymnius, Evenus, and Alcidamas were pupils of Georgias; Theodectes was the pupil of Isocrates.[11] Gradually, then, a corpus of information encompassing highly systematized facts about the theory and practice of rhetoric developed, becoming the formidable discipline of scholastic rhetoric studied in the trivium of the medieval university. It is interesting to note that during the English Renaissance a school rhetoric was revived that had its roots in the pedagogical literature of classical times. It was the work of Aristotle, Cicero, and Quintilian that gave pedagogical consistency to the rhetoric taught in the schools of England.

The teaching of composition in American schools today, unsystematized and fragmented though it may seem, derives directly from the Western classicists through the British masters, Reinolde, Campbell, Blair, and Whately, and through American leaders such as Mather, Adams, Channing, Childs, and Hill. It was the Renaissance in England that focused attention on the Greco-Roman origin of the rhetorical tradition. The works of the masters of rhetoric, Aristotle, Cicero, and Quintilian, were studied in depth and carefully translated for use in the grammar schools. These books became a significant part of the cultural heritage transmitted to future generations. The British *new classicists* of the eighteenth century again looked to the early teachers of rhetoric for guidance in constructing courses of study for English boys in the Latin grammar schools of the day. No better source books were available because no other early rhetors had been copied, translated, and glossed as widely as Aristotle, Cicero, and Quintilian. Furthermore, the classical trilogy, comprehensive and detailed, summarized and explicated the opinions and directives on rhetoric held by notable orators from 500 B.C. to the first century A.D. In historical perspective, then, the philosophical and practical aspects of rhetoric were never far apart.

WHAT CAN RHETORIC DO IN THE K-PH.D. ENGLISH SEQUENCE?

The teaching of rhetoric in today's schools can accomplish several

[11] Freese, John Henry, trans., *Aristotle, The Art of Rhetoric* (Cambridge, Massachusetts: Harvard University Press, 1959), pp. x-ix.

important tasks. Rhetoric's greatest promise is in its power to unify the English program along horizontal and vertical lines from kindergarten to graduate school. Rhetoric can achieve this unity by reiterating the substructural relationships among the English language arts components at successive levels of a student's educational development. Through rhetoric, the student can be brought to use a variety of learning styles related to the *know-that* and *know-how* aspects of his discipline.

Next to language, rhetoric is the single, most important integrative thread in the language arts because the rhetorical method underlies the essayist, the poet, the content of every English component. Thus, the journalist, the literary historian, the news commentator, the dinner speaker, and the linguistic scientist all use a discursive method in sharing their information with society. Even the *belle-lettres* are fundamentally discursive in the design of their intelligibility. Close attention to imaginative literature, to the novel, for example, or to the sonnet, would reveal an unbelievable reliance on persuasive eloquence in the dialogue of characters, for instance, or in the syllogism (enthymeme) underlying the sonnet form.

Rhetoric aptly unifies a multicomponent discipline because *as it functions* it follows the modality of all content in the English discipline, verbal interpretation of reality. Because the characteristic mode of the language arts is verbal interpretation, rhetoric strengthens the structure of the discipline when it functions freely as the *method* of verbal discourse. Students, then, do not learn about the unity of their discipline in an abstract, theoretical way; they *experience* its unity directly as they use the rhetoric of the various components.

Rhetoric is also admirably suited to unify the English curriculum because, like linguistics, its subject matter is the content of the English discipline. True enough, the classical rhetoricians did not agree on the legitimate content of rhetoric, some holding that its proper subject matter was exclusively law and politics. Quintilian, however, protagonist of the tradition from which British and American school rhetoric derive, did not hesitate to say that rhetoric was the science of speaking well about *any subject.* An English teacher would be unwise to direct the teaching of rhetoric to some broad, unrelated content rather than to the rich subject matters of literature, public communication, and linguistics. Through a *functional rhetoric* directed to the content of the English discipline, the student has repeated opportunities to learn the multiple behaviors expected of an English educated man in today's world. Through a functional rhetoric, the student *experiences* the unity of a discipline distinguished by a unique modality, verbal interpretation of reality, and a characteristic method, the rhetorical.

THE PROBLEM OF ORAL AND
WRITTEN COMPOSITION

When rhetoric brings together the divergent streams of oral and written composition, the teaching of English can claim its rightful dignity as an ancient discipline. In the terms identified by Arthur Foshay, professor of education at Columbia University, an English program establishing direct lineage with classical rhetoric can show a definite domain, a characteristic method of dealing with reality and establishing truth, and a history.[12] A rhetoric defining itself as the art of persuasion through discourse, using the characteristic mode of verbal interpretation, and claiming a historicity beyond twenty-five centuries can indeed be called a discipline.

It seems possible that the teaching of rhetoric will obliterate the old, factitious differences between speech and written composition. The best of what has been taught in the speech and dramatics class can, in an integrated rhetoric program, be given to all students at every educational level. If rhetoric is understood to be the *mother discipline* of the English program, the distinctive mode of the language arts, verbal interpretation, is immediately apparent to both teacher and student. Finally, when the venerable history of rhetoric is added to the long past which the English language already boasts, the student of the language can readily understand that the burden he bears, to express himself as accurately as he can, is the burden of an old, old race, patient and long-suffering with the common inadequacy of every language to represent the power and subtlety of the human spirit.

One reason why many teachers and students today find the study of English a fruitless and boring enterprise is because this study, apart from its rhetorical matrix, has degenerated into endless emphasis on disconnected data. Arthur Foshay's criticism of much school subject matter is appropriate here:

> We have become subject-centered in fact; the subject is no longer relevant to the discipline. Our objection to the artificial and largely arbitrary nature of much school subject matter is derived from the fact that it is arbitrary, superficial material. It fails properly to represent the discipline out of which it came.[13]

When a school subject cuts itself off from its proper discipline, it suffers many losses. It sacrifices the wealth of a broader domain; it loses its identification with a tradition; it forfeits the accumlated wisdom in

[12] Arthur W. Foshay, "Education and the Nature of a Discipline," *New Dimensions in Learning: A Multidiscipline Approach* (Washington, D.C.: Association for Supervision and Curriculum Development, 1962), pp. 3-4.
[13] *Ibid.,* p. 5.

the history of the discipline; it becomes rootless, victim of the everchanging exigencies of the present; it becomes formless, adjusting to a temporal flux by adding, changing, and subtracting what is often integral to itself; it becomes purposeless, mistaking the trivial for the important, the proximate for the final, the particular for the universal.

Divorced from their common tradition, both composition and speech have suffered serious setbacks in the English curriculum. Oral work has been reserved for advanced students, and composition has become a purposeless, expository fad. What happened to oral interpretation in the high school? How many junior high school pupils today read orally as part of their experiences in English? Are disadvantaged children permitted to record their ideas on tape to encourage organizational skill while obviating writing deficiencies? Are students at all levels encouraged to write imaginative literature in the traditional forms? Are the subjects students write about worthy of valuable English curriculum time?

Probably the main reason for minimizing oral composition in kindergarten-university English classes is the length of time needed to deliver oral work to an audience. Experienced teachers know that speaking-listening activities cut into curriculum time; their choices, therefore, in the interest of efficiency, favor written work which can be evaluated outside of class. These decisions, while noble, are not forced choices. Other ways to economize on class time without sacrificing students' oral development include such procedures as socialized recitation, group discussion, and multiple tape recording (in language laboratory or multiunits) of individual work.

RHETORIC AND THE INTERRELATIONSHIP
OF THE LANGUAGE ARTS

Certain important emphases made by the classical rhetoricians have great promise for integrating the teaching of English today. One of these emphases is the fact of the interrelationship of the language arts, on which Ruth Strickland has recently reported.[14] Quintilian also discusses this topic, reaffirming what Cicero and rhetoric teachers before him had believed.

> But these rules on style, while part of the student's theoretical knowledge, are not in themselves sufficient to give him oratorical power. In addition he will require an assured facility . . . I know that many have raised the question as to whether this is best acquired by writing, reading, or speaking, and it would indeed be

[14] Ruth Strickland, "The Langauge of Elementary School Children: Its Relationship to the Language of Reading Textbooks and the Quality of Reading of Selected Children," *Bulletin of the School of Education*, Indiana University, Vol. 38 (July, 1961), monograph.

a question calling for serious consideration, if we could rest content with any one of the three. But they are so intimately and inseparably connected that if one of them be neglected, we shall but waste the labour which we have devoted to the others. For eloquence will never attain to its full development or robust health unless it acquires strength by frequent practice in writing, while such practice without the models supplied by reading will be like a ship drifting aimlessly without a steersman.[15]

The classicists, when they spoke of oratory, always inplied a skill that was the outgrowth of proficiency in written composition. All speeches were presumed to be written except one kind, the extemporaneous. Much of the teaching material of the time concerned methods of invention, arrangement, and style. The accomplished orator as well as the student of oratory was judged by the facility he showed in these points of written composition. Of course, there were detailed rules for the memorization and delivery of a speech, but these rules were considered less important than the writing of the speech. Experienced orators were permitted to use notebooks and to refer to them in the courtroom and forum. Quintilian says, however, that the notes Cicero made for his daily cases were so complete that students copied and declaimed them as models of perfectly developed speeches.

As the exhortations of the masters, especially those of Quintilian, show, students were encouraged to write carefully and copiously.

> We must therefore write as much as possible and with the utmost care. For as deep ploughing makes the soil more fertile for the production and support of crops, so if we improve our minds by something more than mere superficial study, we shall produce a richer growth of knowledge and shall retain it with greater accuracy . . . It is in writing that eloquence has its roots and foundations; it is writing that provides that holy of holies where the wealth of oratory is stored, and whence it is produced to meet the demands of sudden emergencies.[16]

In none of the seven books of Aristotle, Cicero, and Quintilian is information about oratory considered to be purely theoretical.

> Our present task is to consider how our athlete, who has learned all the technique of his art from his trainer, is to be prepared by actual practice for the contests in which he will have to engage.
> There can be no doubt that he can accumulate a certain store of resources to be employed whenever they may be required. The resources of which I speak consist in a copious supply of words and matter.[17]

---

[15] Quintilian, *Institutio Oratoria*, IV, Books X-XII, H. E. Butler, trans. (Cambridge, Massachusetts: Harvard University Press, 1959), p. 3.

[16] *Ibid.*, p. 93.

[17] *Ibid.*, p. 5.

Although the techniques of the art are distinguished from the practice of the art, this information is given with a maximum of detail and illustration. It is also given in terms of *know-how* information; that is, the student is addressed as if he will shortly be expected to demonstrate what he has learned. No superfluous or technical information is given which will not be needed for the execution of a technique; neither is any enrichment material such as historical background given, except where the history of conflict over a point seems to clarify it. It is this *functional* aspect of rhetoric that the classicists stressed which serves to give the student an integrated experience with the entire English curriculum.

Of course, rhetoric, like grammar, has a theoretical aspect as well as a functional one. Just as linguistics—the science encompassing language history, language geography, and theories of grammar—can validly be taught as an end-in-itself discipline, so too the forms and methods of rhetoric are a part of communication science. Interesting and appropriate information might include the deliberative, forensic, and epideictic forms of oratory and their corresponding methods of development. Even though this aspect of rhetoric was not stressed in classical times, reaching its full growth in the medieval trivium, the completeness of a course in public communication suggests its inclusion today.

The classicists, interested in practical matters, emphasized handwriting as part of the student's total language education. A good hand was considered a proof of literacy, and the need for dictating to someone was considered a defect in accomplishment. Quintilian writes:

> Writing is of the utmost importance in the study which we have under consideration and by its means alone can true and deeply rooted proficiency be obtained. But a sluggish pen delays our thoughts, while an unformed and illiterate hand cannot be deciphered, a circumstance which necessitates another wearisome task, namely the dictation of what we have written to a copyist.[18]

It is interesting to note that Quintilian followed the opinion of men like Hesiod and Eratosthenes in advocating that children (boys) should be taught to read before they were seven years old. He argued that since children were capable of moral training at an early age they were also capable of literary education. He approved of ivory alphabets which very small children could play with and learn to identify. He suggested a wooden table with the letters dug out so that children could trace over and over the forms with a stylus until the letters or words were learned.

Some of Quintilian's advice on motivating children to love literary study is based on the close interrelationships of the language arts, and might be applicable to the teaching of English today. Students can be stimulated toward verbal efficiency by allowing them to prepare discus-

[18] Quintilian, I, *op. cit.*, p. 35.

sions and speeches on what they enjoy in radio and television shows, in the popular magazines and paperbacks, or in the current musical records.[19] Since each *know-that* component in the English discipline has an experiential counterpart as *know-how* information, a rhetoric that effects the conversion is indispensable. In an English program where rhetoric functions freely, the information presented to the student is *turned into a verbal artifact* bearing the stamp of the individual's personal creative power. Thus, the architecture of the Elizabethan stage becomes a paper model of the Globe Theater which a student explains to the class in a symposium report. The story of Billy Goat Gruff becomes a creative drama in which a small child plays a goat eluding a troll. Psycholinguistic approaches to the problem of style become the dissertation of the prospective Ph.D. When rhetoric is taught efficiently in the English discipline, it becomes the valued *set of instructions* needed by the student to turn theoretical, factual information about English into a creative verbal experience.

SELECTING CONTENT FOR RHETORICAL EXERCISES

An English curriculum is self-integrated to the extent that its content is related to English, its mode is verbal interpretation of reality, and its method is truly rhetorical. As the practice of analyzing protocols for patterns of verbal interchange in the classroom becomes increasingly fruitful, it is becoming apparent that a child can attend English classes for many consecutive days without learning English. The verbal interchange of a given class may be interesting and educative, but it can easily elude the discipline called English.[20] It takes considerable structuring skill on the part of the teacher to plan and execute lessons that genuinely relate to the discipline of English. When teaching and exercising the students in simple narration, argumentation, description, and exposition, it may be wise to use any useful subject matter, keeping the student's attention focused on the method. As soon as possible, however, the vast subject matter of literature, public communication, linguistics, and rhetoric itself should gradually be included as the *subject of the particular method* being taught.

[19] A useful publication on the potential of television products for English teaching is edited by Patrick Hazard, *TV as Art: Some Essays in Criticism* (Champaign, Illinois: National Council of Teachers of English, 1966).

An earlier study suggesting approaches to the problem of intergrating mass media art with a total English program is by Neil Postman, *Television and the Teaching of English* (New York: Appleton-Century-Crofts, 1961).

[20] A useful classification of verbal *moves* in the classroom situation is presented by Arno Bellack, Herbert Kliebard, *et al.*, *The Language of the Classroom* (New York: Teachers College Press, 1966).

TEACHING THE RHETORIC OF NARRATION

The skill of narration, basic to all language activity, is a fundamental technique both in fiction and nonfiction prose. In the short story, the novel, the biography, the historical account, the news article, as well as in the numerous subdivisions of these genres of writing, the technique consists of relating a series of particular actions having sequence, suspense, and a controlling purpose. The four-year-old child seems already to have natural ability in narration. "Mommie, I was riding my bicycle, and Bill came and pulled my shirt and I fell off," is typical of a small child's narrative.

This example is structurally excellent because it relates action (what happened); it is told in sequence; it has suspense or climax; and it reveals a controlling purpose or problem. Generally, children in the first grade can tell interesting narratives, but the slower child often needs help in not getting mixed up (keeping the sequence), and in working toward a climax (having a punch line). The controlling purpose or motive for the narrative is usually the natural need for telling. The elementary school teacher who exercises and develops the child's skill in narration should also clarify the *elements of narration* so that subsequent *know-that* knowledge gained in the junior high school has logical consonance with the *know-how* skills practiced in the elementary school. For example, teachers should not ask children to describe spring or tell about a favorite pet and call this exercise a *story. Only when a narration has the four requisite elements of action, sequence, suspense, and purpose should it be called a story.* When children are reasonably sure of the technique, the integration with traditional subject matter in the English discipline should be begun.

Integration has often been effected successfully in prenarrative teaching by having the student *retell* a fable or short story he has heard or read. Socialized recitation, working in groups, and using recording equipment all facilitate this practice in the classroom. Writing from dictation and copying short narratives are also forms of retelling that facilitate the child's development of skill in handling the elements of narration. Young children enjoy copying, exchanging, and retelling jokes, narratives in miniature.

One exercise that especially delights middle grade children asks them to give the *prose statement* of a narrative poem. Humorous poems best suit this exercise because if the element of climax is not caught in the retelling, the story "falls flat," lacking the humorous punch line anticipated by the audience. American literature is rich in appropriate selections for this exercise.

Creating is probably the most satisfying kind of exercise the child will experience in developing narrative skill, though retelling is usually enjoyed when exercises are shared by a sympathetic listening audience. The writing of stories can be fictive (imaginative) or real. Both are important and valid exercises in narration, and both should be used repeatedly to foster genuine skill. Integration with *know-that* information in the English discipline can be effected by having characters, situations, and moral acts in parallel or contrast with those of stories studied.

THE RHETORIC OF ARGUMENTATION

It seems strange that a skill in composition, which some modern textbooks regard as a highly sophisticated ability, Quintilian regarded as next to narration in order of complexity. The classicists regarded argumentation as an adjunct of narration, for, as they held, "much that is said can be disputed." Perhaps the general inability of American children today to read and write critically stems from the neglect of exercises in argumentation in the language arts program. To think critically does not mean to think negatively, for confirming is as essential to criticism as refuting. The skills involved in both confirmation and refutation include judging a thing, supporting the judgment, and expressing the judgment. For this reason Quintilian taught argumentation in conjunction with narration, and literary criticism has always been the art most closely associated with literature.

Small children seem to judge things naturally, saying for instance, "I love peanut butter," or "He's bad." In spite of the fact that these judgments are about nonliterary things, they are valid expressions of the child's power to criticize or evaluate reality in his own terms. With direction, a child's ability to evaluate can be extended to include the verbal interpretations other persons have made of reality. The first step is to train him to judge the conditions of the expression: their truth or falsity, their probability or appropriateness; then the quality of the expression: its value insofar as he sees it; then his personal feelings regarding the original expression. For example, a child might tell the following story.

The Monkey Who Learned to Fly

Horace was the tiniest monkey in his family. Everyone else was gayly swinging from tree to tree, but Horace always fell in between the branches, and it hurt him too. His mother scolded him because he was so clumsy and his father scolded him because he was so stupid and his brothers and sisters scolded him because he never could keep up with them. One day Horace said to himself, "I wish I could fly." He wished so hard that soon he felt himself getting higher and higher off the ground. He flapped his arms a little, straightened out his tail, and soon he was sailing high above the jungle trees. All the monkeys in the jungle saw him. His mother and father and brothers and sisters saw him and everyone said,

"Just look at Horace! He is the smartest monkey in the jungle."

Such a story might suggest the following key remarks on the part of the teacher.

Tommy made up a fine story, didn't he? Were you glad that Horace learned to fly? Why? Do monkeys usually fly? How do they get around? Are there any parts of the story you would like to hear again? Which parts? Why? Did Tommy tell the story well? What did he do to make it enjoyable? Why did you like this story?

With the younger children in the primary grades the teacher assumes the major responsibility of leading the children to judge the *what, why,* and *how* of narration, giving the students the greatest freedom in expressing likes or dislikes. At no time, however, should a preferential judgment be accepted without an accompanying reason, even if the teacher at first supplies plausible reasons himself.

In the intermediate grades the skill of marshalling evidence or proof for the *what, why,* and *how* of narration should be taught and practiced daily. Frequent occasions present themselves not only in the reading lessons but also in the content of the English discipline which should be taught there. The best experiences are those which are both written and oral. Here again, group discussion is a valuable timesaver.

At the junior and senior high school level no expression of likes and dislikes should be accepted in the English classroom unless it is validly substantiated by some kind of evidence. It is not necessary that students be taught a special course in logic to support their statements, though a knowledgeable teacher can easily teach inductive and deductive reasoning and what Aristotle called the "popular syllogism," the enthymeme. It is usually useful to the high school student to recognize fallacious reasoning and propaganda tricks. He enjoys identifying such devices as misinterpretation of statistics, mistaking the cause, begging the question, rationalization, circular reasoning, false alternatives, hasty generalization, reasoning by analogy, and the *non sequitur.* He enjoyes discussing such advertising tricks as the bandwagon appeal, the personal endorsement, the appeal to worthy emotion (the soft-soap), the plain folks' appeal, and others. Ordinarily the student should not be given exercises in constructing these kinds of arguments, though the assignment of an occasional parody helps to insure his mastery of *know-that* data. It is best for students not to be exercised in verbal chicanery. They should, however, be given frequent experience in expressing their judgments on a variety of things, especially on other persons' opinions and interpretations of facts.

One important point of emphasis at every level of instruction, except the primary, is that responsible persons base their judgments of reality on fact. Attitudes, values, and emotions are facts of human existence, and students would be misguided not to recognize and use them as bases of judgment, whether that judgment be a direct evaluation of reality or an assessment of another's verbal interpretation. A second point of emphasis must be that just as narration has a controlling purpose, to tell, so too argumentation has a controlling purpose, to convince.

THE RHETORIC OF DESCRIPTION

Although description is considered an easy exercise in some modern textbooks, editors suggesting it as one of the ways to develop paragraphs, Quintilian recommended that it be the third general exercise in the teaching of rhetoric. Only after the student had made considerable progress in exercising and expressing judgment, Quintilian believed, should he come to important descriptive writing. Although the classicists required some argumentative practice as a prerequisite for a particular kind of descriptive writing which they called epideictic (the praise or blame of famous persons), the principle of having judgment precede description seems to be a sound one. Before children are actively aware of their environment and of their power to judge and interpret it in their own terms, it is unlikely that they will show genuine descriptive prowess.

Although the word *description* is used loosely to mean explanation (to "describe" a process), or narration (to "describe" an event), or even argumentation (to "describe" an opinion or theory), it has a specific definition of its own when it is used in the teaching of rhetoric. Here descriptive writing means that an author *has stated in words* his sensory experience of particular things in the world of phenomena. He tells what he sees, feels, hears, tastes, touches, or imagines.

Description, then, can be either scientific or artistic. If scientific, it usually attempts to give an exact, terse account of what is observed or measured. If artistic, it gives a verbal account, marked by literary excellence, of real or imagined phenomena. In the first case, the writing is objective; in the second, subjective. It is precisely here that the English discipline *in its entirety* becomes the subject matter of a *functioning* rhetoric. Scientific description is admirably suited to each student's particular power of interpreting the *know-that* information of a particular lesson. By listening to the student's interpretation the teacher can assess the extent and the manner in which a student has understood facts about English. Artistic description is admirably suited to develop the individual student's creative power. The rigor of scientific learning can be enhanced by encouraging artistic interpretation. Because the literary artist uses both rhetorical methods in his verbal production, the student can only profit from experiencing simultaneously both the discipline and freedom of his English subject matter.

Since it is easy to confuse description with other methods of writing, the elementary school teacher might well use specific objects when asking students to practice description. She might, for instance, supply tulips as objects of factual description. The following composition would be one of factual description.

The Tulip

A tulip is a flower that looks like a deep cup without a handle. It has two rows of petals, inside petals and outside petals. The three inside petals fold over each other a little. The three outside petals cover the place where the inside ones touch. Deep inside the cup there is a short part that stands straight up. Around this there are six little stems that have a kind of black powder on them. There is no nice smell to a tulip but it looks pretty because it comes in any color, even pure black.

The elementary school teacher must also make a point of distinguishing factual description of this kind from imaginative representation. Children in the second and third grades usually distinguish fact from fancy. One simple way to keep the factual and imaginative clear for the young child is to encourage him to use the personal pronouns in his artistic compositions and to omit *I* and *we* in his factual reports. Because the same basic skill of describing is needed, however, the teacher might use real objects to suggest composition but then remove them so that the child must reconstruct the sensory experience by using his imagination. An exercise in imaginative description might begin with concrete objects. A bowl of tulips, for example, might result in a composition similar to the following.

Tulip Buds

I love tulip buds because they look like delicious lollipops on long sticks. The red ones are cherry, the yellow ones are lemon, the orange ones are orange, and the black ones are licorice. The red one is so pretty I can almost taste it.

Exercises in description should ordinarily be short because this kind of writing is seldom useful in its pure form. Mixed with narration, argumentation, and exposition, it brings the dimension of sense experience to all verbal interpretation, thus clarifying and enriching it. When students have had little training in this method of writing at the elementary level, it may be advisable for the junior or senior high school teacher to provide instruction and specific practice before assigning topics for composition which demand skill in several writing methods. Even at the secondary level care must be taken that description is not confused with narration. By controlling the assignment, that is, by suggesting topics which exclude the describing of actions or events, and by choosing models carefully, the teacher can facilitate the development of specific skills. If the varied talents of children are to be fostered through the language arts program, however, both kinds of description, factual and artistic, must be encouraged.

THE RHETORIC OF EXPOSITION

Quintilian and the other classicists recommended that comparison, one of the elements of exposition, be taught after some skill in description had been acquired. This seems logical for it is impossible to describe the relationship of two things if the qualities of one cannot be described. Exposition, which also includes definition, analysis, classification, exemplification, comparison, and casual relationships, is the last skill to be taught in a patterned composition program because it is the most difficult. Exposition demands intellectual precision and a persistent intention, two skills difficult for the novice to master.

Most expository writing is vitiated because it is imprecise. Students at every level need intellectual discipline in order to delineate carefully a plan, a purpose, a method, a condition. If the subject is trivial, such as how to tie your shoe, the second characteristic of good exposition is negated, persistent intention. Because the rhetorical intention of all expository writing is to inform, the writing is purposeless if the audience already knows what is to be conveyed. In the classroom, true exposition is impossible if students are not required to explain subjects which are foreign to the other members of the class. Whereas other methods of writing can be ingeniously devised, expository writing is tied to the facts of reality. This limitation makes it necessary for a writer to execute his work in a disciplined and precise way and to maintain the genuine intention of informing. If an exposition is inexact or deals with a subject commonly known to an audience, it is purposeless.

Because the younger the child the less precise he is intellectually and the less interested in assuming the genuine responsibility of instructor, exercises in exposition may be delayed until some mastery in narration, argumentation, and description has been demonstrated. Expository exercises, whether in definition, analysis, classification, exemplification, or causality, are probably inappropriate below grade four. Here they should be introduced only when students have shown ability in using the other methods of writing. In the junior high school, all methods should be taught and practiced, the expository included, so that students are skilled enough to allow the senior high school teacher sufficient scope in the planning of exercises. Though the eighth or ninth grade pupil may write exposition poorly, he must nevertheless submit to the discipline of this method of writing in the hope that he will develop the skills with which expository writing is concerned, namely intellectual astuteness and a responsible intention to inform. The genuine interest of his subject matter should serve to distract him from the rigors of logical expression.

THE PROBLEM OF FRESHMAN COMPOSITION

It seems that a good many educators have arbitrarily assigned the mode of expository writing to the unique scrutiny and practice of college freshmen. *New Design,* however, holds that level 14 and 15, the lower biennium in college, can profit as much from information and experience in a total curriculum as any of the lower levels. Skill in expository writing can be improved by practicing it in combination with other basic styles of writing. Furthermore, there is considerable information in the total English discipline which has never been explored by the college student. This subject matter often fits an interpretive mode other than exposition. There seems to be little reason for confining the freshmen and sophomore subject matter to a single mode of writing about miscellaneous subject matter.

Logically, the English education of the first two years of college (sometimes the English component of the junior college curriculum) ought to reiterate the basic design of a four-component, self-integrated curriculum. Courses in major literary figures and various literary genre sometimes given at the sophomore level need the matrix of the total English discipline in order to function in a maximally efficient way in the student's personal growth in verbal interpretation of reality.

COMPOSITION AND LOGIC:
HISTORICAL DEVELOPMENT

In its long history of development, the relationship of rhetoric to logic has been both asserted and challenged. Although the art of using language to achieve a desired effect was first used by Corax of Syracuse in 466 B.C. in legal proceedings, it was thought to be different from logic because it emphasized the manner of the speaker rather than the matter or method of the procedure. However, because the claimants for property lacked documentary support and relied chiefly on inferential reasoning, the relationship of rhetoric and logic is rather clearly established.[21] Be-

[21] "Rhetoric," *Encyclopedia Britannica*, Vol. 19 (1963), p. 247.

sides giving rules for the arrangement of the five parts of a good *case,* proem, narrative, arguments, subsidiary remarks, and peroration, Corax also took pains to illustrate the use of the argument of general probability, one of the basic logical procedures.

Rhetoric was not essentially changed, although a variety of forms and functions were added in the period between Corax and Aristotle. Tisias, the pupil of Corax, and subsequent intellectual figures such as Plato, Lysias, Antiphon, and Isocrates brought the use of rhetoric to the perfection of a highly complex art.[22]

It was Aristotle (384-322 B.C.) who in his monumental work, *De Rhetorica,* asserted that dialectic (logic) and rhetoric constitute the dual art of discourse. He developed rules for the use of rhetoric as the popular branch of logic. Claiming that "the master of logic will be the master of rhetoric," Aristotle, nevertheless, seemed to realize that speakers without the ghost of an argument, by the skillful use of language, might carry large audiences.

The tradition of ornateness, ostentatious display, and general affectation in speech which clings to the development of rhetoric as an art was originally an Asian influence that took deep root at Rome, where it found many enthusiastic imitators around the second century B.C. Two schools developed, the ornate and the purist. The Attic school, named for Attica, a state in ancient Greece whose capital was Athens, defended the simple, classical, restrained style. It was this school that Hermagorus of Temnas (c110 B.C.) followed in establishing the scholastic rhetoric that dominated medieval education and subsequently influenced English and American education.

Under Marcus Aurelius, Hermogenes of Tarsus made a complete digest of scholastic rhetoric which helped this art to dominate the first four centuries of the Roman Empire while other arts were degenerate. The law courts of the numerous subdivisions of Roman provinces created continual demand for forensic speaking. The early fathers of the Catholic church relied heavily on rhetorical skill for the dissemination and acceptance of the Christian religion. Probably the first great Christian rhetoric is found in St. Augustine's fourth book of *De Doctrina Christiana.* Augustine (himself trained in rhetoric before his conversion) held that the logical groundwork underlying rhetoric and the "last embellishment" should be brought to the defense and perpetuation of the new doctrine.[23]

During the Renaissance, new interest in classical learning, especially in England, revived the best teaching of the ancients and introduced into the British universities (Cambridge, 1570; Oxford, 1588) a rhetoric that

---

[22] *Ibid.,* p. 248.

[23] Kenneth Burke, *A Rhetoric of Motives* (New York: Prentice-Hall, Inc., 1950), p. 53.

had gained remarkable strength and clarity by its association with logic in the medieval universities.[24] In 1620, George Herbert, the metaphysical poet who, like his colleagues, made apt use of rhetorical devices in his work, held the office of public orator at Cambridge.

Although rhetoric flourished in seventeenth century England, its decay set in when logic, its mainstay, deserted to the camp of the new scientific investigation. Here logic was used to formulate the canons of induction, to deny the primacy of the syllogism, and generally to supply the appealing coherence of the scientific method.[25] Stripped of its muscle, rhetoric might well have deserved Waterland's cryptic remark (1732):

> Take but away their rhetorications and equivocal expressions and their cause will be left in a manner destitute.[26]

In spite of the divorce between academic rhetoric and logic, the principles and tropes of effective rhetoric continued to be used by literary figures of both the Romantic and Victorian eras. Coleridge, Wordsworth, Newman, and Macaulay are a few writers whose work exemplifies a careful rhetorical method based on logic.

In eighteenth and nineteenth century America, the development of rhetoric suffered no lag. Logic and rhetoric were united in the instructional program at Harvard, Princeton, and Bowdoin, where students were trained exclusively for the ministry, for law, or for political service. Early textbooks in rhetoric were few, the most widely used being Hugh Blair's *Lectures on Rhetoric* (1783).[27] This Scottish manual was superseded by Richard Whately's *Elements of Rhetoric* (Dublin, 1834).

In his preface to this text, Whately clarified his position on the logic versus rhetoric controversy:

> I propose in the present work to adopt a middle course between these two points . . . considering Rhetoric (in conformity with the very just and philosophical view of Aristotle) as an offshoot from Logic.[28]

This tradition continued until 1911 when a committee of the National Education Association merged with a group from the newly formed National Council of Teachers of English to broaden the scope and objectives of English to meet the social diversity of the population. In a reorganization that pointed the English curriculum away from the need of

---

[24] W. Rhys Roberts, *Greek Rhetoric and Literary Criticism* (New York: Longmans, Green and Company, 1928), p. 52.

[25] Donald C. Bryant, ed., *The Rhetorical Idiom* (New York: Cornell University Press, 1958), p. 56.

[26] *Oxford English Dictionary*, Vol. VIII (1933), p. 627.

[27] "Rhetoric," *Americana*, Vol. 23 (1961), p. 458.

[28] Richard Whately, *Elements of Rhetoric* (London and New York: James Monroe and William Jackson Companies, 1834), p. 5.

the college-bound student for grammar, literature, and composition and toward the general educative needs of the masses, rhetoric and its old companion logic were lost entirely. In the 1935 radical revision of the curriculum where *life adjustment* and *experience* were the key ideas, the last traces of rhetoric-logic as an academic discipline integral to the teaching of communication were obliterated.

Today, the relationship between rhetoric and logic has received little scholarly attention from English educators. However, as transformational grammar theory seeks to explore the deep structure of thought beneath the syntactical level of verbal expression, so too rhetoric will come to consider once more the relationship between discourse and the pattern of reasoning.[29] The modern discipline of psycholinguistics, by bringing together the study of personality and the study of verbal behavior, promises to reunite rhetoric and logic.[30]

DEVELOPING A PERSONAL VERBAL STYLE

Since verbal behavior is generally accepted as the index of a person's inner self, growth in self-identity and power in verbal expression is revealed by speech and writing. It is important that even young children are encouraged to use a personal, creative style in creating their verbal products. Writing and speaking in the wide variety of forms available in the tradition of verbal art, and studying and valuing the characteristic styles of many literary men of distinction help the student to develop his own individuality.

When the basic modes of discourse have been taught and the fundamental techniques of verbal expression have been learned, there is little for the teacher to do except to motivate the student toward ever greater perfection. Skill and artistry in verbal self-expression are endlessly perfectible, and like every art they need not be the subject of endless instruction. Quintilian describes as follows the ever increasing independence students ought to gain:

> Beginners must be given a subject sketched and ready for treatment and suitable to their respective powers. But when they show that they have formed themselves sufficiently close to the models placed before them, it will be sufficient to give them a few brief hints for their guidance and to allow them to advance trusting in their own strength and without external support. Sometimes they should be left entirely to their own devices that they may not be spoilt by the bad habit of always relying on another's efforts,

[29] See Noam Chomsky, *Aspects of the Theory of Syntax* (Cambridge, Massachusetts: The M.I.T. Press, 1965).

[30] John B. Carroll, *The Study of Language* (Cambridge, Massachusetts: Harvard University Press, 1966), p. 111.

and so prove incapable of effort and originality. But as soon as they seem to have acquired a sound conception of what they ought to say, the teacher's work will be near completion: if they still make some mistakes they must be brought back under his guidance.[31]

The classicists realized that the art of composition is a highly personal one. When a student has mastered the basic principles and methods of the art under the direction of a competent teacher, there is little more to be done except to practice and refine his skill. Even in their training of individual students, the classicists recognized various degrees of potential talent, and took these into account as they worked with individuals.

When Ralph Waldo Emerson said, "A man's style is his mind's voice," he was asserting the unique quality of each writer's work. As students work with functional elements of the English curriculum, they will come to a realistic knowledge of their strengths and limitations in verbal art. Self-awareness and self-confidence develop in students when teachers accept individual verbal profiles, encouraging the development of skill commensurate with the student's individual talent and ambition. When the resources of a total English curriculum are used to develop a student's verbal creativity from kindergarten upward, there needs to be little concern for illiteracy. A functioning rhetoric will assist a child in achieving a satisfying style of verbal expression appropriate to his age and talent.

Besides unifying the multicomponent English curriculum, then, the study of rhetoric can effect a meaningful liaison between the student and the discipline called English. When this has been accomplished, the English teacher has adequate proof of his effectiveness; when the student cannot make personal creative interpretations of reality, the English teacher has failed.

As the English teaching profession moves forward, research in the measurement of children's verbal performance will become increasingly proficient. Today, the profession does not have adequate tests of multiple verbal behaviors at any of the K-Ph.D. levels. The equating of reading competency with total language facility has created serious problems for both teachers and students in the English teaching profession. When fundamental performance skills in speaking are ignored in language testing, curriculists tend to minimize the value of oral communication in favor of written skills in the building of English curriculums. Such a distortion penalizes the children for whom reading and writing is difficult and bars them from using a major learning resource, oral language. More and more, the teaching of English to poorly languaged children shows a high correlation with improvement in oral English.

[31] Quintilian, *Institutio Oratoria*, I, *op. cit.*, pp. 259-261.

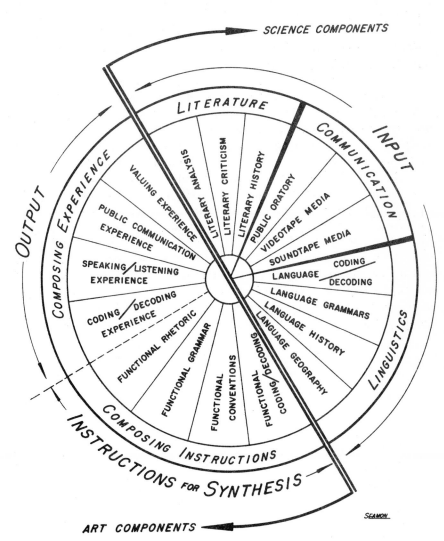

Figure 13. *The English curriculum in technical terms.*

If the major objective in the teaching of English is *the improvement of personal creative verbality*, it might be well for future research in the profession to look at the process of English education in somewhat technical terms. Figure 13 shows how the *know-that* components in the English discipline might be considered as computer *input*. Before a desired *output* of verbal products can be achieved, the individual needs instructions for synthesizing subject matter into desired combinations.

Thus, the *output* depends on the *input* and *instructions for synthesis*. Of course, the individual variables of talent and motivation make each verbal product a highly unpredictable kind of output. The analogy between student and computer, however, signals the teacher to provide adequate *know-how* information and experience if he expects the *know-that input* to result in a student's demonstrated verbal competency.

The discipline of rhetoric, that discipline which traditionally concerned itself with excellence in verbal performance, is the foundation of the language arts. Man's need to communicate effectively both in speech and writing is the motive for teaching rhetoric in the K-Ph.D. English curriculum. By means of rhetoric, the factual information in the discipline, and indeed in all reality, becomes the subject matter of personal verbal creativity. When rhetoric is taught from kindergarten to graduate school, the English discipline becomes unified and relevant through the individual's power to create and express its meaning. English is at once the subject matter, the mode, and the verbal art product of an individual.

VII

Notes for the English Supervisor

The major commitment of the English supervisor is the personal-professional development of English teachers. This key responsibility inheres in the fact that in education the supervisory process is an extension of the classroom instructional process. Expressed simply, the supervisor's job is to improve classroom learning; but this is impossible to accomplish without improving the *chief structuring agent* of the classroom teaching-learning situation, the teacher. The supervisor's main task, then, is to improve the teacher. Since all persons are self-actualizing entities, the supervisor's role can only be defined in terms of a cooperating agent in the improvement of classroom instruction. The English supervisor's role is to help English teachers develop personally and professionally so that they become more effective educational agents in the classroom.[1]

Whether an English supervisor works at the kindergarten or college level, he must always be a specialist in the discipline he supervises. According to the consistency of *New Design,* the supervisor is *a teacher who was a student in the English discipline.* Ideally, the supervisor should be a Ph.D. product of the K-Ph.D. sequence in English education, but this is not always practical or necessary. Depending upon the range of his professional work, the academic preparation of his teachers, the special problems of his student population, and many other variables, the supervisor may terminate his English education at an appropriate level before the Ph.D. and yet be sufficiently trained in the eighteen component discipline to serve the needs of his teachers. Common sense would dictate, however, that the level of his own English education exceed that level to which he hopes to bring his teachers. The main requirement of an English supervisor's education is that it be a multicomponent education, if

[1] Mary Columbro, "Supervision and Action Research," *Educational Leadership,* Vol. 21 (February, 1964), pp. 297-300.

Figure 14. *The English student, embodiment of a multicomponent English discipline.*

he is to supervise a multicomponent program. The English supervisor, then, must be *himself* a product of a multicomponent English curriculum.[2] Figure 14 represents the English student, an embodiment of the eighteen components in the English discipline. An English supervisor who lacks *know-that* or *know-how* information in some area of English cannot pretend to help a teacher requesting assistance in that particular area. The old truism, *no one gives what he does not have,* applies here.

In addition to being a student educated in a multicomponent English discipline, the supervisor must also be a teacher, trained in the teaching of English. This means that, besides his knowledge and experience in the English discipline as a student, the supervisor needs the educational psychology and English teaching methodology courses that teachers receive. Academic studies in the psychology of learning at a variety of levels prepare a supervisor to handle problems in actual field situations; courses in English teaching methodology prepare supervisors to solve instructional problems in teaching the *know-that* and *know-how* information encompassed by the English discipline. Figure 15 depicts the English teacher implicit in every English supervisor.

Like all instructional personnel in English, the supervisor is well aware of the basic difference between the *know-how* of a curriculum subject and the *know-how* of *teaching* that subject. It is one thing, for example, to know and use the method of literary criticism, and it is quite another to know and use a *method of teaching* teachers to structure learning situations to communicate that knowledge and skill in the classroom. In the first instance the supervisor is a student, competent in *knowing* the scientific aspects of a particular English component and experienced in *using* his information in a personally creative verbal mode. In the second instance the supervisor is a teacher (as well as a student), competent in his *knowledge* of methods of teaching a particular component and also experienced in *teaching* according to that method. In other words, the behaviors of the English teacher are a set of behaviors *different* from those of the English student. The supervisor needs them both.

There has been endless confusion about English methods because a clear distinction is seldom made between the *method or mode of an English component* (disciplinary method) and the *instructional method* of teaching a particular segment of the discipline. In the first instance, whoever is involved is a *student.* He is studying and practicing the mode of the novelist, for example, or the literary critic, or the linguist. He is

---

[2] English supervisors today will necessarily be products of an *informal* multicomponent English education. Like teachers who have not had an opportunity to take academic courses in linguistics, communication, and the new rhetoric, being forced to learn the information independently, supervisors will need to fill their own subject matter gaps in a variety of ways.

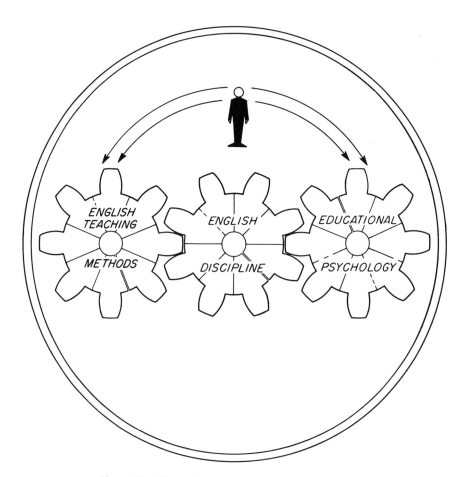

Figure 15. *The well-prepared K-Ph.D. English teacher.*

implementing the method *by which the discipline developed;* he is adding something to the content of the discipline. In the second instance, whoever is involved is a teacher. He is studying and practicing methods great teachers have used to structure effective learning situations; he is adding something new to instructional method. In each instance the set of behaviors is different; the person involved is different. Disciplinary method (or mode) is for students; instructional method is for teachers.

Recent research in English education has fairly well disproved the notion that a knowledge of English content insures instructional success in that area. The question about who should teach the English methods course, the college of arts and sciences or the college of education, can be answered if the distinction between disciplinary mode and instructional method is understood. English departments teaching the content subject should be responsible for exercising the student in the mode (or modes) characteristic of his discipline; education departments giving professional training should provide study and practice in instructional methods related to a discipline. A responsibility not yet felt by some schools of education is that of organizing courses in instructional methods[3] for college and graduate school teachers. Though a number of major universities in the United States have established graduate departments of English Education precisely for this purpose, the teacher of the content subject in college and graduate school seems to reject professional training of this kind.

The English supervisor is necessarily an expert in both English and education. He must know and use the content of his discipline, and he must also know and use the instructional method of his discipline. Because all instructional method is suspect unless the teacher has a clear understanding of learning theory, the supervisor's training must include educational psychology at an appropriate level. In addition to psychology, the supervisor's preparatory studies should include English methodology and English supervision. Figure 16 shows how the *professional* components of a supervisor's preparation might be integrated with his total English education. By comparison with Figure 15, the construct in Figure 17 shows that the English supervisor's preparation is identical with that of the English teacher, except in the one component of supervision. Levels at which professional training should be introduced for both English teachers and English supervisors will vary in particular programs. *New Design* holds that the professional courses should precede actual practicing experience. Figure 17 is a graphic depiction of the English supervisor well prepared to supervise the English program at any level from kindergarten to graduate school. The supervisor who has been

---

[3] Educational research is implicit in instructional methodology in the same way that library research is implicit in literary scholarship.

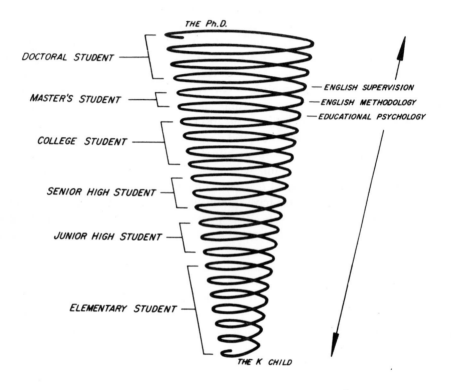

THE Ph.D.

DOCTORAL STUDENT

MASTER'S STUDENT —ENGLISH SUPERVISION
—ENGLISH METHODOLOGY
—EDUCATIONAL PSYCHOLOGY

COLLEGE STUDENT

SENIOR HIGH STUDENT

JUNIOR HIGH STUDENT

ELEMENTARY STUDENT

THE K CHILD

Figure 16. *The professional components in English education.*

trained as a student and as a teacher in the English discipline will be best qualified to help teachers develop their personal-professional competencies.

SPECIAL PROBLEMS IN ENGLISH SUPERVISION

Not all English teachers are prepared for effective work in their field. The National Council of Teachers of English has noted that "between 40 and 60 percent of the English in our public junior and senior high schools is being taught by teachers who lack even the minimal training required for a major in English."[4] Squire and Hogan also report that nonmajors in English make less effort to overcome their deficiencies than majors, avoiding advanced courses in language, literature, composition, and communication.[5] It is generally known that few K-6 language arts teachers take advanced undergraduate or graduate work in English.

The underprepared English teacher is sometimes the product of poorly conceived English teacher preparation programs. The National Council of Teachers of English reports that three out of five English majors and three out of four English minors are not required to complete advanced courses in composition.[6] The recommendation of James B. Conant that fifty percent of high school English courses be devoted to composition is made in vain when only thirty-three percent of the present national English staff is adequately prepared to teach even basic composition.[7] The National Association of Secondary School Principals emphasizes that "during each school semester, provision must be made to teach writing systematically, sequentially, and continuously,"[8] but this is an impossibility for teachers who are not familiar with rhetoric and its provisions for cumulative growth in writing skill. Elementary school teachers are often required to take a minimum of only nine semester hours of English in their academic program, and many cannot qualify for further course work in the four major components of their discipline.

Professional training for English teachers is similarly lacking in many instances, a result of narrowly conceived teacher preparation pro-

[4] James R. Squire and Robert F. Hogan, "A Five Point Program for Improving the Continuing Education of Teachers of English," *Bulletin of the National Association of Secondary School Principals*, Vol. 48 (February, 1964), p. 6.

[5] *Ibid.*, p. 16.

[6] Committee on National Interest, *The National Interest and the Teaching of English* (Champaign, Illinois: The National Council of Teachers of English, 1961), p. 70.

[7] James B. Conant, *The American High School Today* (New York: McGraw-Hill, Inc., 1960), pp. 50-51.

[8] *"English Language Arts in the Comprehensive Secondary School,"* National Association of Secondary School Principals (Washington: National Education Association, 1960), p. 6.

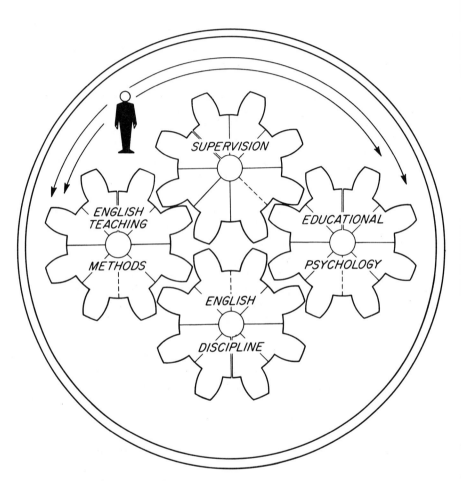

Figure 17. *The well-prepared K-Ph.D. English supervisor.*

grams. English methods courses and courses in educational psychology are often omitted for future teachers at every educational level. According to Squire and Hogan,[9] 25 percent of the present English teaching staff in grades 7-12 has not completed *any course work in education.* James B. Conant observed that teachers on the job do not tend to make up what collegiate programs lacked; their choices among extension courses, miscellaneous and unrelated to needs, could result in fragmentary, haphazard learning.[10]

The problem of inadequately prepared teachers is complicated by the tidal wave of new knowledge in the four areas of the English discipline. With insufficient background in his discipline, the English teacher is seriously threatened by the new information and materials being unable to understand and evaluate it. This situation suggests several tasks for the English supervisor.

ARRANGING INSERVICE ACADEMIC COURSES

In the recent national survey of the continuing education of teachers, the most highly rated inservice activity is the college course.[11] Three values associated with these courses are their specificity, their acceptance by school boards for salary increments, and their accompanying academic credit. Whereas almost a third of the nation's secondary English teachers report that less than 10 percent of the institutes which they attend are devoted to instruction in English, there is no complaint about courses chosen freely at evening and summer schools.[12] There is a growing demand for course work in the new linguistics, in rhetoric, in practical literary criticism, and in mass communication.

One of the supervisor's main tasks is to assist in organizing courses which teachers need to advance academically and professionally. Working with local college and university department heads of English and education, supervisors must create practical consonance between what the university offers in its catalogue of courses and what the teachers have expressed as their genuine needs. There are often serious discrepancies. Supervisors can be instrumental in having academic courses taught at convenient hours and in classrooms easily accessible to teachers. University campuses are often far removed from the locales of teachers taking the courses. Supervisors can also help college teachers modify a traditional course content to meet the needs of a group of teachers lacking

---

[9] James R. Squire and Robert F. Hogan, *op. cit.*, p. 3.
[10] James B. Conant, *The Education of American Teachers* (New York: McGraw-Hill, Inc., 1963), pp. 191-192.
[11] James R. Squire and Robert F. Hogan, *op. cit.*, p. 15.
[12] *Ibid.*, p. 12.

prerequisite courses, or to organize new courses for teachers who need them. A supervisor who completed his training in the K-Ph.D. English curriculum might well request appointment as a visiting faculty member of several universities, and teach academic or professional courses needed by teachers for college or graduate school credit in certain geographical areas.

ORGANIZING CONFERENCES AND WORKSHOPS

Supervisors can waste the professional time of teachers by poorly focused inservice activities. If an activity is intended to give the teacher a personal-professional competency or experience, it should be carefully organized to meet that end. Teachers resent endless work on committees for curriculum revision and textbook selection. When their experience and insight is needed in these matters, it should be requested as a professional favor and not exploited. The busywork of typing and mimeographing curriculums and courses of study and the task of ordering books should be done by secretaries.

To help provide challenging activities in the teaching of English, supervisors should explore the resources of nearby colleges and schools of education. In the NCTE survey, 49.9 percent of the secondary teachers said they had never had an opportunity to confer on curriculum or planning with a college specialist in English, and over 50 percent had never been able to work with an English education specialist.[13] Since there are approximately thirteen hundred institutions of collegiate and university rank in the United States, and the count increases by 50 percent if junior and community colleges are counted, supervisors should be able to establish useful contacts with academic departments of English and education.

When teacher conferences and workshops are planned to include leading scholars and educators, much can be accomplished in keeping teachers abreast of new developments in the field. On-the-job professional activities promote teacher growth if they are planned in consonance with the genuine needs of teachers. Interdisciplinary workshops are often necessary within a school system to achieve certain goals cooperatively. However, teachers need conferences and workshops *in the subject matter of English* where they can work out specific problems pertinent to their field. Two-thirds of the secondary English teachers surveyed in the recent study by the National Council of Teachers of English complained that only about 50 percent of overall institute time ever dealt with the subject matter that they taught.[14]

[13] *The English Journal,* Vol. LIII (April, 1964), p. 4.
[14] James R. Squire and Robert F. Hogan, *op. cit.,* p. 12.

RECOMMENDING ACADEMIC AND
PROFESSIONAL ORGANIZATIONS

Because English education includes several distinct areas of subject matter, the supervisor should promote membership in both academic and professional organizations related to the teaching of English. When one member of a staff keeps abreast of some area such as linguistics, or poetry criticism, or methodology in English, the whole staff gains from his comments and insights. Some teachers have the time and talent to keep up with both academic and professional interests. To encourage teachers to belong only to the National Education Association or to one section of the National Council of Teachers of English is hardly enough in a modern world enriched with the products of mass media communication. The talented, well-trained teacher should be guided toward maximum involvement in his professional work.The Shakespeare Society, the Linguistic Society of America, Theater Crafts, American Poetry Society, the National Library Association, Speech Society of America, state forensic leagues, state education associations, and similar groups are worthy of any English teacher's membership and interest. The duty of the supervisor is to bring these possibilities to the attention of his staff members and to demonstrate their value through his own interest and involvement.

ORGANIZING PROFESSIONAL LIBRARIES

Teachers need specialized libraries where they can find the latest and best books concerning their work. Whether the books are kept in a special faculty section of the school library, in the English department office, or in the teachers' lounge, they must be *easily accessible*. Collections in offices at the curriculum center in a school district are not easily accessible, and books are apt not to be read and discussed as they would be in individual school libraries.

Titles in the English teachers' professional library should include yearly publications by the National Council of Teachers of English, subject matter books requested by teachers, appropriate journals of educational research, and outstanding publications in the field of English teaching generally. The department chairman might well consider it his responsibility to keep the collection consonant with teachers' developing interests, and often ask his teachers which particular books, journals, or materials they might wish to use. Teachers might be asked to report their assessment of certain titles at English department meetings.

GUIDING ACTION RESEARCH

When the supervisor promotes action research he promotes an objective analysis of classroom problems. He also calls upon the creative talent of individual teachers to solve the problems they identify. The spirit of inquiry which action research stimulates is probably the greatest single factor in initiating change in teaching methods. There is unquestionably a need for innovation, if school practices are to come abreast of what is valid knowledge in the field of English education. Squire and Hogan report on the reluctance of English teachers to try new things:

> A survey of the nation's secondary school English teachers unveils the startling paucity of experimentation with new patterns of instruction: not more than 11.8 percent of the nation's English teachers working with programed instruction, not more than 10 percent involved in team teaching, only 7 percent utilizing lay readers, only 3.1 percent experimenting with ungraded teaching.[15]

When supervisors provide training for teachers in action research they build the spirit of inquiry, foster creative action, and provide the tools with which teachers can solve the problems that annoy them.

Supervisors must realize that action research is a new and integrated approach to knowing. It is an approach that recognizes the objective, scientific process of research and the inner subjective experiences of the researcher.[16] Ross L. Mooney writes:

> We want a way of holding assumptions about research which makes it possible to integrate the pursuit of science and research with the acceptance and fruitful development of one's self.[17]

By providing training in action research, supervisors can help teachers become aware of their own power to initiate change in education. Stephen Corey states:

> Most of the study of what should be kept in the schools, what should go, and what should be added must be done in hundreds and thousands of classrooms in thousands of American communities.[18]

The supervisor, then, should be aware that there are five major kinds of inservice activities to help teachers develop the competency they need

[15] *Ibid.*, p. 2.

[16] Abraham Shumsky, "Learning about Learning from Action Research," *Learning and the Teacher* (Washington, D.C.: Association for Supervision and Curriculum Development, 1957), p. 187.

[17] Ross L. Mooney, "The Researcher Himself," *Research for Curriculum Improvement* (Washington, D.C.: Association for Supervision and Curriculum Development, 1957), p. 166.

[18] Stephen Corey, *Action Research to Improve School Practices* (New York: Bureau of Publications, Teachers College, Columbia University, 1953), p. 8.

to teach a multicomponent English program: academic courses, workshops and conferences, academic and professional organizations, professional libraries, and action research. Supervisory leadership in promoting these programs is guided by the supervisor's own understanding of the conceptual framework of an integrated English program. Unless the supervisor sees the interrelationships of a multicomponent program and can explicate the rationale of such a program, he cannot lead others to knowledge and implementation. Unless the English supervisor is *a teacher who was a student* in the four component English discipline, he can, at best, hope only for a modicum of success.

A CONCLUDING STATEMENT

The work of conceptualization is a dynamic, creative one. The supervisor is never finished refining a theoretical model of an English curriculum because language is an everchanging phenomenon. If the facts of language change, then the theories of language must change, for as Emmon Bach says, "linguistic theories are sets of statements about language."[19] New language theories must be incorporated in curriculum models if English instruction is to be based on valid information. Not only the facts of language, but also the forms, techniques, and styles of verbal art are in constant evolution. Verbal art is highly individualistic, and each writer adds the distinction of his own creative talent to the form through which he chooses to express his vision of reality. When Paul Roberts says, "Grammar is the heart of language, and language is the foremost of the features that make human beings human," he points up the unique quality of expression which every man has.[20] It is this quality that precipitates change in literary technique, in style, and ultimately in form. The English supervisor's work is to keep abreast of new developments and to help the classroom teacher adjust the curriculum design to meet the needs of his students.

Conceptualization in so complex a process as curriculum design implies cooperative action. When the supervisor accepts a leadership role in a subject area such as English, his main duty is to learn and to promulgate new developments in the field which are suitable to the needs of his group. All the creative talents of his staff are needed to arrive at a refined conceptualization of a curriculum design needed for a particular district or a particular classroom.

English educators should be reasonable in expecting curriculum building from supervisory personnel. At any level, the job of curriculist

[19] Emmon Bach, *An Introduction to Transformational Grammars* (New York: Holt, Rinehart and Winston, Inc., 1964), p. 2.

[20] Paul Roberts, *English Sentences* (New York: Harcourt, Brace and World, Inc., 1962), p. 4.

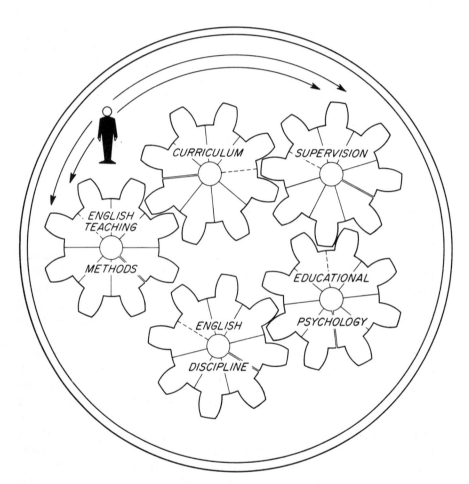

Figure 18.   *The well-prepared English curriculist.*

demands both professional time and training. Figure 18 shows the complex of preparatory subject matter needed by a well-trained English curriculum specialist. The additional studies needed beyond those of a supervisor qualify the curriculist to handle the sociological and economic problems related to the development of curriculums for special groups of students.

Ordinarily a supervisor is wholly involved in the improvement of instructional methodologies and in the personal-professional growth of teachers. It seems unrealistic both from the standpoint of training and from the standpoint of professional time limitations to require curriculum organization of a detailed nature. The supervisor as subject specialist and as colleague of his teachers is a reservoir of information about implementing curriculums in particular schools or districts. Because his professional judgments are based on both a knowledge of the discipline and a knowledge of the English staff's strengths and needs, he ought to serve in an advisory capacity on all subjects related to curriculum development projects in a school or district. He ought not, however, be charged with the major responsibility of curriculum design. This kind of work is in the curriculist's domain and requires advanced training.

Doctoral programs and post-Master specializations can provide the professional education courses required for either supervisory practice or curriculum development. When English in its entirety as a discipline is taught in a kindergarten to graduate school sequence, an English major has ordinarily achieved a strong command of his discipline by level seventeen or eighteen. Several courses in English teaching methods are required here for all professional personnel in English education. These courses in instructional methods are offered by either education departments or English education departments. The students in these methods courses are elementary, secondary, college, or graduate school teachers of English. A series of required methods courses should include the special methodologies implicit in a multicomponent English discipline: teaching literature and literary criticism, teaching mass oral communication, teaching language and linguistics, teaching rhetoric and composition.

When all English teaching personnel have studied instructional methods, their professional focus is on the primacy of the teaching-learning act. Depending on the interests of the individual, further academic and professional course work toward advanced graduate specialties or doctoral degrees prepare students for careers in teaching, supervision, or curriculum. When the English teaching profession has a unified conceptual understanding of the English discipline and of the English education structure needed to transmit that discipline, students at every educational level can be guaranteed improvement in verbal power.

Bibliography

Allport, Floyd H., *et al. Written Composition and Characteristics of Personality: An Experiment.* New York: Syracuse University Press, 1934.

Anderson, H. A. *Creativity and Its Cultivation.* New York: Harper and Brothers, 1959.

Andrews, Michael F. *Creativity and Psychological Health.* New York: Syracuse University Press, 1960.

Aristotle. *The Art of Rhetoric,* trans. by John Henry Freese. Cambridge, Massachusetts: Harvard University Press, 1959.

Association for Supervision and Curriculum Development. *Perceiving, Behaving, Becoming.* Washington, D.C.: ASCD, 1962.

———. *Research for Curriculum Improvement.* Washington, D.C.: ASCD, 1957.

Ausubel, David P. *The Psychology of Meaningful Verbal Learning.* New York and London: Grune and Stratton, 1963.

Bach, Emmon. *An Introduction to Transformational Grammars.* New York: Holt, Rinehart and Winston, Inc., 1964.

Baird, A. Craig. *Rhetoric, A Philosophical Inquiry.* New York: The Ronald Press, 1965.

Baldwin, Charles S. *A College Manual of Rhetoric.* New York: Longman's, Greene, and Company, 1907.

Ballard, Philip Boswood. *Thought and Language.* London: University of London Press, 1934.

Barnett, Walter W. *A Study of the Effects of Sentence Diagraming on English Correctness and Silent Reading Ability.* Unpublished master's thesis, University of Iowa, 1942.

Bateman, Donald and Frank Zidonis. *The Effect of a Study of Transformational Grammar on the Writing of Ninth and Tenth Graders.* Champaign, Illinois: National Council of Teachers of English, 1966.

163

Bellack, Arno A., *Theory and Research in Teaching*. New York: Teachers College Press, 1963.

Bellack, Arno A., Herbert Kliebard, *et al. The Language of the Classroom*. New York: Teachers College Press, 1966.

Bernstein, Abraham. *Teaching English in High School*. New York: Random House, Inc., 1961.

Blair, Hugh. *Lectures on Rhetoric and Belles Lettres*. (2 volumes). London: (fourth edition). 1790.

Bloom, Benjamin S., ed. *Taxonomy of Educational Objectives, Handbook I: Cognitive Domain*. New York: David McKay Company, Inc., 1956.

Bloomfield, Leonard. Review of Edward Sapir's *Language in the Classical Weekly*, Vol. XV (1922).

Bluem, A. William, ed. *Mass Media and Communication*. New York: Hastings House, Publishers, 1966.

Boutwell, William D., ed. *Using Mass Media in the Schools*. New York: Appleton-Century-Crofts, Inc., 1962.

Broudy, Harry S. and John R. Palmer, *Exemplars of Teaching Method*. Chicago: Rand McNally and Company, 1965.

Brownell, John A. "Becoming Three-Story Men," *English Education Today*, Dwight L. Burton, ed. Champaign, Illinois: National Council of Teachers of English, 1963.

Bruner, Jerome S. *The Process of Education*. Cambridge, Massachusetts: Harvard University Press, 1961.

Bryant, Donald C., ed. *The Rhetorical Idiom*. New York: Cornell University Press, 1958.

Burgh, James. *The Art of Speaking*. Baltimore: Printed for Samuel Butler, 1804.

Burke, Kenneth. *A Rhetoric of Motives*. New York: Prentice-Hall, Inc., 1950.

Burton, Dwight L. *Literature Study in the High Schools*. New York: Holt, Rinehart and Winston, Inc., 1964.

Burton, Dwight L. and John S. Simmons, eds. *Teaching English in Today's High Schools*. New York: Holt, Rinehart and Winston, Inc., 1966.

Cairns, William B. *The Forms of Discourse*. New York: Ginn and Company, 1897.

Campbell, George. *The Philosophy of Rhetoric* (3 volumes). London: Printed for W. Strahan and T. Cadell, 1776.

Carlsen, G. Robert. "Deep Down Beneath, Where I Live," *English Journal*, Vol. XLIII (May, 1954), pp. 235-239.

———. "The Way of the Spirit and the Way of the Mind," *College English*, Vol. 24 (February, 1963), pp. 333-338.

Carroll, John B. *The Study of Language.* Cambridge, Massachusetts: Harvard University Press, 1966.

Chomsky, Noam. *Aspects of the Theory of Grammar.* Cambridge, Massachusetts: The M.I.T. Press, 1965.

————. *Cartesian Linquistics.* New York: Harper and Row, 1966.

————. *Syntatic Structures.* The Hague: Mouton and Company, 1963.

Cicero. *Ad Herennium,* trans. by Harry Caplan. Cambridge, Massachusetts: Harvard University Press, 1959.

————. *De Inventione,* trans. by H. M. Hubbell. Cambridge, Massachusetts: Harvard University Press, 1959.

Columbro, Mary Nazaire. *A Conceptual Framework for the Teaching and Supervision of High School English.* Columbus, Ohio: The Ohio State University (unpublished doctoral dissertation), 1964.

Commission on English of the College Entrance Examination Board. *The National Interest and the Teaching of English.* Champaign, Illinois: The National Council of Teachers of English, 1961.

————. *Freedom and Discipline.* New York: College Entrance Examination Board, 1965.

Commission on the English Curriculum, National Council of Teachers of English. *An Outline of Desirable Outcomes and Experiences in the Language Arts,* Communication No. 7. Chicago: National Council of Teachers of English, 1949.

————. *The Education of Teachers of English.* New York: Appleton-Century-Crofts, Inc., 1963.

————. *The English Language Arts.* New York: Appleton-Century-Crofts, Inc., 1952.

————. *The English Language Arts in the Secondary School.* New York: Appleton-Century-Crofts, Inc., 1956.

Conant, James B. *The American High School Today.* New York: McGraw-Hill, Inc., 1960.

————. *The Education of American Teachers.* New York: McGraw-Hill, Inc., 1963.

Cooke, Increase. *The American Orator; or Elegant Extracts in Prose and Poetry; Comprehending a Diversity of Oratorical Specimens.* New Haven: John Babcock and Son, 1818.

Coppee, Henry. *Elements of Rhetoric; Designed as a Manual of Instruction.* Philadelphia: E. H. Butler and Company, 1859.

Corey, Stephen. *Action Research to Improve School Practices.* New York: Bureau of Publications, Teachers College, Columbia University, 1953.

Crosby, Muriel. *Supervision as Cooperative Action.* New York: Appleton-Century-Crofts, Inc., 1957.

Curry, S. S. *Foundations of Expression: Studies and Problems for De-*

veloping the Voice, Body, and Mind in Reading and Speaking. Boston: The Expression Company, 1927.

Dale, Edgar. "Quotable," *The Nation's Schools,* Vol. 56 (August, 1955). pp. 32-35.

Day, Henry N. *The Art of English Composition.* New York: Charles Scribner and Company, 1867.

————. *Rhetorical Praxis: The Principles of Rhetoric.* Cincinnati: Moore, Wilstach, and Baldwin, 1850 and 1860.

Deer, Irving and Harriet A. Deer, *The Popular Arts, A Critical Reader.* New York: Charles Scribner's Sons, 1967.

DeBoer, John J. "The Concept of Creativity in Reading," *Perspectives on English, Robert C. Pooley,* ed. New York: Appleton-Century-Crofts, Inc., 1960.

Dinneen, Francis P., S.J. *An Introduction to General Linguistics.* New York: Holt, Rinehart and Winston, Inc., 1966.

Eberhart, Wilfred J. *The Teaching of Functional Grammar in the Secondary School.* Columbus, Ohio: The Ohio State University (unpublished doctoral dissertation), 1936.

Eberhart, Wilfred J., *et al. Manual for Reading-Literature,* Book Three. New York: Row, Peterson and Company, 1950.

Eliot, T. S. "Tradition and the Individual Talent," *Selected Essays.* New York: Harcourt, Brace and World, Inc., 1932.

Fillmore, Charles J. *Disentential Complement Verbs in English.* The Ohio State University Research Foundation, GN 174. April, 1964.

Fliegler. *Creativity and Psychological Health.* New York: Syracuse University Press, 1961.

Fodor, Jerry A. and Jerrold J. Katz, eds. *The Structure of Language: Readings in the Philosophy of Language.* Englewood Cliffs, New Jersey: Prentice-Hall, Inc., 1964.

Foshay, Arthur W. "Education and the Nature of a Discipline," *New Dimensions in Learning: A Multidisciplinary Approach.* Washington, D.C.: Association for Supervision and Curriculum Development, 1962.

Franseth, Jane. *Supervision as Leadership.* Evanston, Illinois: Row, Peterson and Company, 1961.

Frazier, Alexander, ed. *New Insights and the Curriculum.* Washington, D.C.: Association for Supervision and Curriculum Development, 1963.

Fries, Charles Carpenter. *Linguistics and Reading.* New York: Holt, Rinehart and Winston, Inc., 1963.

————. *American English Grammar.* New York: Appleton-Century-Crofts, 1940.

————. *The Structure of English.* New York: Harcourt, Brace and Company, 1952.

Frye, Northrop. *Anatomy of Criticism.* Princeton, New Jersey: Princeton University Press, 1958.

————. "Literary Criticism," in *The Aims and Methods of Scholarship in Modern Languages and Literatures.* New York: Modern Language Association, 1963.

Frymier, Jack R. *The Nature of Educational Method.* Columbus, Ohio: Charles E. Merrill Books, Inc., 1965.

Gage, N. L., ed. *Handbook of Research on Teaching.* Chicago: Rand McNally and Company, 1963.

Galfo, Armano J., and Earl Miller, *Interpreting Educational Research.* Dubuque, Iowa: Wm. C. Brown Company, 1965.

Genung, John F. *Handbook of Rhetorical Analysis.* New York: Ginn and Company, 1888.

Genung, John F. and Charles Lane Hanson, *Outlines of Composition and Rhetoric.* New York: Ginn and Company, 1915.

Getzels, Jacob W., and Philip W. Jackson, *Creativity and Intelligence.* London and New York: John Wiley and Sons, Inc., 1962.

Gibbony, Hazel L. *Enrichment: A Classroom Challenge.* Columbus: F. J. Heer Printing Company, 1962.

Gleason, Henry Allan, Jr. *Linguistics and English Grammar.* New York: Holt, Rinehart and Winston, Inc., 1965.

Goldberg, Maxwell H. "General Education and the Explosion of Knowledge," *College and University Bulletin,* Vol. 14 (February 1962), pp. 3-5.

Good, Carter V. *Introduction to Educational Research.* New York: Appleton-Century-Crofts, Inc., 1963.

Goodlad, John I. "Toward a Conceptual System for Curriculum Problems," *The School Review,* Vol. LXIV (Winter, 1958), pp. 391-401.

Gray, J. Stanley. *Communicative Speaking.* Boston: The Expression Company, 1928.

Greene, Harry A. "Direct versus Formal Methods in English," *Elementary English Review,* Vol. 14 (1937), pp. 189-225.

Guth, Hans P. *English Today and Tomorrow.* Englewood Cliffs, New Jersey: Prentice-Hall, Inc., 1964.

Hafner, Lawrence E., ed. *Improved Reading in Secondary Schools.* New York: The Macmillan Company, 1967.

Hatfield, Wilbur and Walter Barnes, "The Situation as Regards English," *A Modern Curriculum in English.* Washington, D.C.: NEA, Department of Supervisors and Directors of Instruction, 1936.

Householder, F. W. "On Linguistic Terms," *Psycholinguistics.* New York: Holt, Rinehart and Winston, Inc., 1961.

Hazard, Patrick, ed. *TV As Art: Some Essays in Criticism.* Champaign, Illinois: National Council of Teachers of English, 1966.

Healy, Katharine L. "A Study of the Factors Involved in the Rating of

Pupils' Composition," *Journal of Experimental Education,* Vol. IV (September, 1935), pp. 50-53.

Heilman, Robert B. "Literature and Growing Up," *English Journal,* Vol. XLV (September, 1956), pp. 303-313.

Herbert, John. *A System for Analyzing Lessons.* New York: Teachers College Press, 1966.

Hill, Abraham. *Lectures on Rhetoric and Belles Lettres Chiefly from the Lectures of Dr. Blair.* New York: George R. Lockwood, 1832.

Hill, Adams Sherman. *The Principles of Rhetoric.* New York: Harper and Brothers, 1897.

Hill, David J. *The Elements of Rhetoric.* New York: Sheldon and Company, 1878.

————. *The Science of Rhetoric.* New York: Sheldon and Company, 1877.

Hinton, Eugene Mark. *An Analytical Study of the Qualities of Style and Rhetoric Found in English Compositions.* New York: Columbia University Contributions to Education, No. 806, 1940.

History and Criticism of American Public Address (2 volumes). New York: McGraw-Hill Book Company, Inc., 1943.

Hocker, Mary Elsa. *Reading Materials for Children Based on Their Language Patterns of Syntax, Vocabulary, and Interests.* University of Arizona, (unpublished master's thesis), 1963.

Hook, J. N. *The Teaching of High School English.* New York: The Ronald Press, 1965.

————. *Writing Creatively.* Boston: D. C. Heath and Company, 1963.

Hoyt, Franklin S. "The Place of Grammar in the Elementary Curriculum," *Teachers College Record,* Vol. 7 (1906), pp. 1-34.

Hunt, Kellogg W. *Grammatical Structures Written at Three Grade Levels.* Champaign, Illinois: National Council of Teachers of English, 1965.

Ives, Sumner. "Grammar and Composition," *Readings in Applied English Linguistics,* Harold B. Allen, ed. New York: Appleton-Century-Crofts, Inc., 1958.

Johnson, Neal F. *Linguistic Models and Functional Units of Language Behavior.* The Ohio State University, 1964.

Jespersen, Otto H. *The Philosophy of Grammar.* New York: Henry Holt and Company, Inc., 1924.

The Journal of Aesthetic Education. Inaugural Issue (Spring, 1966), Champaign Illinois: University of Illinois.

Kaulfers, Walter V. "Common Sense in the Teaching of Grammar," *Elementary English Review,* Vol. 21 (1944), pp. 168-174.

Kitzhaber, Albert R. *Themes, Theories, and Therapy: The Teaching of Writing in College.* New York: McGraw-Hill Book Company, Inc., 1963.

Klapper, Joseph. *The Effects of Mass Media.* New York: Bureau of Applied Research, Columbia University, 1949.

Krathwohl, David R., Benjamin S. Bloom, and Bertram B. Masia. *Taxonomy of Educational Objectives, Handbook II: Affective Domain.* New York: David McKay Company, Inc., 1964.

LaBrant, Lou. *We Teach English.* New York: Harcourt, Brace and Company, 1951.

Lazarsfeld, Paul F. *Communication Research.* New York: Harper and Row, 1949.

Lazarus, Arnold and Rozanne Knudson. *Selected Objectives for the English Language Arts.* Boston: Houghton Mifflin Company, 1967.

Lees, Robert B. "The Grammar of English Nominalizations," *International Journal of American Linguistics,* Vol. 26 (July, 1960), monograph.

Loban, Walter. *The Language of Elementary School Children.* Champaign, Illinois: National Council of Teachers of English, 1963.

————. *Problems in Oral English.* Champaign, Illinois: National Council of Teachers of English, 1966.

Loban, Walter, Margaret Ryan, and James R. Squire. *Teaching Language and Literature.* New York: Harcourt, Brace and World, Inc., 1961.

Lotz, John. "Linguistics: Symbols Make Man," *Psycholinguistics.* New York: Holt, Rinehart and Winston, Inc., 1961.

Lowenfeld, Viktor. *Creativity and Psychological Health.* New York: Syracuse University Press, 1961.

Macdonald, James B. "The Nature of Instruction: Needed Theory and Research," *Educational Leadership,* Vol. 21 (October, 1963), pp. 5-7.

Marckwardt, Albert H. *Linguistics and the Teaching of English.* Bloomington, Indiana: Indiana University Press, 1966.

Marsh, John. *Blair's Lectures on Rhetoric and Belles Lettres Reduced to Question and Answer.* Hartford, Connecticut: Samuel G. Goodrich, 1820.

Maslow, Abraham H. *Motivation and Personality.* New York: Harper and Brothers, 1954.

McLuhan, Marshall Herbert. *Understanding Media.* New York: McGraw-Hill Book Company, 1964.

Meckel, Henry C. "Research on Teaching Composition and Literature," *Handbook of Research on Teaching,* N. L. Gage, ed., American Educational Research Association. Chicago: Rand McNally and Company.

Menyuk, Paula. *Syntactic Structures in the Language of Children.* Boston University (unpublished doctoral dissertation), 1961.

Mooney, Ross L. "The Researcher Himself," *Research for Curriculum*

Improvement. Washington, D.C.: Association for Supervision and Curriculum Development, 1957.

Moulton, William G. "Linguistics," *The Aims and Methods of Scholarship in Modern Languages and Literature*. New York: Modern Language Association, 1963.

National Association of Secondary School Principals. *English Language Arts in the Comprehensive Secondary School*. Washington, D.C.: National Education Association, 1960.

National Council of Teachers of English. *The Basic Issue in the Teaching of English*. Supplement of *College English*, Vol. 48 (October, 1959).

————. *Conducting Experiences in English*. New York: Appleton-Century-Crofts, Inc., 1939.

————. *Reading in an Age of Mass Communication*. English Monograph No. 17. New York: Appleton-Century-Crofts, Inc., 1949.

————. *The National Interest and the Continuing Education of Teachers of English*. Champaign, Illinois: National Council of Teachers or English, 1964.

National Education Association. *Teacher Supply and Demand in Universities, Colleges, and Junior Colleges, 1959-1960 and 1960-1961*. Higher Education Series, Research Report 1961-R-12. Washington, D.C.: NEA, 1961.

Newman, Samuel P. *A Practical System of Rhetoric: or the Principles and Rules of Style, Inferred from Examples of Writing*. Portland: Shirley and Hyde, 1829.

Nutting, Rufus. *A Grammar of the English Language*. Montpelier, Vermont: E. P. Walton and Sons, 1840.

O'Donnell, Roy C., William J. Griffith, and Raymond C. Norris, *Syntax of Kindergarten and Elementary School Children: A Transformational Analysis*. Champaign, Illinois: National Council of Teachers of English, 1967.

Peacham, Henry. *The Garden of Eloquence*. London: H. Jackson, 1577. Facsimilie reference copy, Huntington Library. Microfilm copy, University Microfilms, Inc., Ann Arbor, Michigan, 1963.

Pearce, Roy Harvey. "Literature, History, and Humanism," *College English*, Vol. 24 (February, 1963), pp. 364-372.

Pei, Mario. *Glossary of Linguistic Terminology*. New York: Columbia University Press, 1966.

————. *Tex and Reference Books in Rhetoric Before 1750*. Chicago: private edition, distributed by University of Chicago Libraries, 1940.

Plato. *The Phaedrus*, W. C. Helmbold and W. G. Rabinowitz, trans. Indianapolis, Indiana: Liberal Arts Press, Bobbs-Merrill Company, 1958.

Pollock, Thomas Clark. "Transmitting our Literary Heritage, *English Journal,* Vol. 31 (January, 1942), pp. 200-210.

Pooley, Robert C., ed. *Perspectives on English.* New York: Appleton-Century-Crofts, Inc., 1960.

Postman, Neil. *Television and the Teaching of English.* New York: Appleton-Century-Crofts, Inc., 1961.

Quackenbos, J. D. *Practical Rhetoric.* New York: American Book Company, 1896.

Quintilian. *Institutio Oratorio,* I, Books I-III; II Books IV-VI; III, Books VII-IX; IV, Books X-XIII. trans H. M. Hubbell. Cambridge, Massachusetts: Harvard University Press, 1959.

Rainolde, Richard. *The Foundacion of Rhetorique.* London: Ibon Kingston, 1563; New York: Scholars' Facsimiles and Reprints, 1945.

Reid, Paul E. "The Boylston Chair of Rhetoric and Oratory," *Western Speech,* Vol. 3 (Spring, 1960), pp. 83-89.

Richards, I. A. *The Philosophy of Rhetoric.* New York: Oxford University Press, 1936.

———. *Practical Criticism.* New York: Harcourt, Brace and Company, 1929.

Riling, Mildred E. *Oral and Written Language of Children in Grades 4 and 6 Compared with the Language of Their Textbooks.* Report to the U.S. Office of Education, Cooperative Research Project No. 2410, 1965.

Rivlin, Harry N. *Functional Grammar,* unpublished doctoral dissertation, Teachers College, Columbia University, No. 435.

Roberts, Paul. *English Sentences.* New York: Harcourt, Brace and World, Inc., 1962.

———. *English Syntax: A Book of Programmed Lessons.* New York: Harcourt, Brace and World, Inc., 1964.

Roberts, W. Rhys. *Greek Rhetoric and Literary Criticism.* New York: Longman's, Green and Company, 1928.

Rodgers, Mary Columbro. *State Supervision of English and Reading Instruction.* Champaign, Illinois: National Council of Teachers of English, 1967.

Rogers, Carl. *On Becoming a Person.* Boston: Houghton Mifflin Company, 1961.

Rogovin, Syrell. *Modern English Sentence Structure.* New York: Random House, 1964.

Runkel, Philip J. "Cognitive Similarity in Facilitating Communication," *Sociometry,* Vol. 19 (1956), pp. 178-191.

Russell, David H. *Children Learn to Read.* New York: Ginn and Company 1961.

Sam, N. H. and Stine. *Structural Analysis of the Written Composition of Intermediate Grade Children,* Report to the U.S. Office of Education, Cooperative Research Project No. S-057, 1965.

Sapir, Edward. *Language: An Introduction to the Study of Speech.* New York: Harcourt, Brace and Company, 1921.

Sauer, Edwin H. *English in the Secondary School.* New York: Holt, Rinehart and Winston, Inc., 1961.

Schramm, Wilbur. *Communication in Modern Society.* Urbana, Illinois: University of Illinois Press, 1948.

———. *Mass Communication,* 2nd edition. Urbana, Illinois: University of Illinois Press, 1960.

Schramm, Wilbur. *et al.* "Patterns in Children's Reading of Newspapers," *Using Mass Media in the Schools.* New York: Appleton-Century-Crofts, Inc., 1962.

Scott Fred Newton and Joseph Villiers Denny. *The New Composition—Rhetoric.* Boston: Allyn and Bacon, 1911.

Searles, John R. and G. Robert Carlsen. "Language, Grammar, and Composition" *Encyclopedia of Educational Research,* Chester W. Harris ed., American Educational Research Association. New York: Macmillan Company, 1960.

Shattuck, Marquis and Walter Barnes. *The Situation as Regards English.* Washington, D.C.: Department of Supervisors and Directors of Instruction, National Education Association, 1936.

Sheridan Marion C. "The Teaching of Literature in Secondary Schools," *Perspectives on English,* Robert C. Pooley, ed. New York: Appleton-Century-Crofts, Inc., 1964.

Sherry, Richard. *A Treatise of Schemes and Tropes.* London: John Day, 1550. Manuscript copy, Bodleian Library, Oxford: *A Facsimile Reproduction* by Scholars' Facsimiles and Reprints, Gainsville, Florida, 1961.

Shumsky, Abraham. "Learning about Learning from Action Research," *Learning and the Teacher.* Washington, D.C.: Association for Supervision and Curriculum Development, 1957.

Shurter, Edwin DuBois. *The Rhetoric of Oratory.* New York: Macmillan Company, 1909.

Sledd, James. *A Short Introduction to English Grammar.* Chicago: Scott, Foresman, and Company, 1959.

Slobin, Dan. *Grammatical Transformations and Sentence Comprehension in Childhood and Adulthood.* Harvard University (unpublished doctoral dissertation), 1963.

Smith, Dora V. *Selected Essays.* New York: The Macmillan Company, 1964.

Smith, John. *The Mysterie of Rhetorique Unvail'd.* London: Printed by

E. Cotes for George Eversden, 1657. Reproduction, Ann Arbor, Michigan, University Microfilms, 1962.

Spiller, Robert E. "Literary History," *The Aims and Methods of Scholarship in Modern Languages and Literatures.* New York: Modern Language Association, 1963.

Squire, James R., and Robert F. Hogan. "A Five Point Program for Improving the Continuing Education of Teachers of English," *Bulletin of the National Association of Secondary School Principals,* Vol. 48 (February, 1964), pp. 1-17.

Steinberg, Charles, ed. *Mass Media and Communication.* New York: Hastings House, Publishers, 1966.

Stone, George Winchester, Jr. *Issues, Problems, and Approaches in the Teaching of English.* New York: Holt, Rinehart and Winston, Inc., 1961.

Strickland, Ruth G. "Evaluating Children's Composition" *Children's Writing: Research in Composition and Related Skills.* Champaign, Illinois: National Council of Teachers of English, 1960.

———. *The Language Arts in the Elementary School.* Boston: D. C. Heath and Company, 1957.

———. "The Language of Elementary School Children: Its Relationship to the Language of Reading Textbooks and the Quality of Reading of Selected Children," *Bulletin of the School of Education,* Indiana University, Vol. 38 (July, 1962), monograph.

Taba, Hilda. *Curriculum Development.* New York: Harcourt, Brace and World, Inc., 1962.

Taylor, Calvin W. "A Tentative Description of the Creative Individual," *Human Variability and Learning.* Washington, D.C.: Association for Supervision and Curriculum Development, 1961.

Torrance, E. Paul. *Guiding Creative Talent.* Englewood Cliffs, New Jersey: Prentice-Hall, Inc., 1962.

Torrance, E. Paul, *et al. Assessing the Creative Thinking Abilities of Children.* Minneapolis: Bureau of Educational Research, University of Minnesota, 1960.

Trager, George and Henry Lee Smith, *An Outline of English Structure.* Reprinted, Washington, D.C.: American Council of Learned Societies, 1957.

Tyler, Ralph W. *Basic Principles of Curriculum and Instruction.* Chicago, Illinois: University of Chicago Press, 1962.

Tuttle, Donald R. *Curriculum Patterns in English.* Washington, D.C.: U.S. Government Printing Office, 1965.

Utley, Francis Lee, *et al. Bear, Man, and God.* New York: Random House, 1964.

Vygotsky, L. S. *Thought and Language.* Eugenia Hanfmann and Gertrude Vakar, trans. New York: Massachusetts Institute of Technology and John Wiley and Sons, Inc., 1962.

Ward, John. *A System of Oratory* (2 volumes). London: (no printer given), 1759. Facsimile reproduction, Library of Congress microfilm, 1962.

Waterman, John Thomas. *Perspectives in Linguistics.* Chicago: University of Chicago Press, 1963.

Welleck, René and Austin Warren, *Theory of Literature.* New York: Harcourt, Brace and Company, 1942.

Webster, Noah. *An American Selection of Lessons in Reading and Speaking Calculated to Improve the Minds and Refine the Taste of Youth.* New Haven: David Hogan, 1809.

Wimsatt, William K., and Cleanth Brooks. *Literary Criticism: A Short History.* New York: Alfred A. Knopf, Inc., 1957.

Whately, Richard. *Elements of Rhetoric.* Oxford: W. Baxter, fourth edition, 1832.

White, Helen C. *Changing Styles in Literary Studies.* Cambridge: Cambridge University Press, 1963.

Whitehead, Alfred North. *The Aims of Education.* New York: The Macmillan Company, 1929.

Willing, Matthew H. *Valid Diagnosis in High School Composition.* Teachers College, Columbia University Contributions to Education, No. 230. New York: Columbia University Press, 1926.

Wilson, Thomas. *The Arte of Rhetorique.* London: Richard Grafton, 1553. Manuscript copy in Newberry Library: *A Facsimile Reproduction* by Scholars' Facsimiles and Reprints, Gainsville, Florida, 1962.

Wimsatt, W. K. Jr. "What to Say About a Poem," *College English,* Vol. XXIV (February, 1963), pp. 377-383.

Index